The machine age started early in Corrinne. One turn of the crank with a $2.50 gold piece in the slot got the lawyers' client a divorce . . . and a turn of the crank was about all murder boss Stanton needed to kill a man. There was Alex MacDonald of Dawson City who found so much gold it took twenty-nine mules to pack it to town, and Daniel Kern who found that not all that glitters is gold, and that the silver sides of a salmon could found an industry and the town of Kernville, Oregon.

What about the "Black Gold" of the Kemerer Coal Mining Company of Wyoming and the "Wooden Gold" in the giant Douglas Firs of the Washington forests?

It's the glorious 4th time around for that restless hunter of the hidden hills, Lambert Florin. He puts ghost towns in three categories but his readers put him in a category all his own for finding forgotten places and photographing them as no one else can. His ghost town sense and picture making skill improves with each passing sandstorm and his volume of readers increases with each volume he brings forth.

In GHOST TOWN SHADOWS author Florin catches up on some **IN** Arizona, Nevada, Utah and Oregon ghosts he missed earlier, ack called to his attention by amateur hunters and people in the local- ks, ities, and now he invades the famed Yukon Territory. Here he ide unearths nuggets out of the Rush to the Klondike and photographs not the forlorn remains of many fabulous camps such as Clear Creek, rn- Dawson City, Whitehorse, Skagway and Bennet, B.C. . . . and ro- brings to life such fantastic characters as Jefferson Randal in (Soapy) Smith, One-Eyed Riley, Ed Scheffelin of Tombstone, nd Arizona, and the same Sam Magee, from Plumtree, Tennessee, who never did get warm.

This is Florin at his finest, picturing the ghostly relics of dramatic ny days with canny detail and chinking up the spaces between with as colorful tales of gold strikes and honkytonks and frail sisters and ag- moonstruck miners . . . all treasure for every reader. the ho

tonks? — where did they go when the town died?"

GHOST TOWN

SHADOWS

Western
GHOST TOWN
Shadows.

BY LAMBERT FLORIN

THESE WEATHERED BUILDINGS still stand in Dawson City, Yukon Territory, Canada. Originally an Indian fishing village at the confluence of the Yukon and Klondike Rivers, the place boomed to a city of 30,000 miners and opportunists in a short time. It was the capitol of Yukon Territory for many years. Fading with the decline of gold mining, Dawson City has become a museum piece, full of relics of one of the most fantastic gold rushes of all time.

SUPERIOR PUBLISHING COMPANY-SEATTLE

GHOST TOWN TRAILS

is dedicated to David C. Mason, M.D.,
whose help and encouragement
have made this book possible.

FOREWORD

The concept that a ghost can be classified may come as a surprise. Genuine wraiths are somewhat out of our field, but over a period of years, many thousands of miles of travel and much research, it is evident there is seldom a clear-cut definition of a ghost town. We would place ghost towns in three categories — the very dead, the not-so-dead and the lively.

In the first group would fall those that are mere sites, with nothing remaining to indicate a once lusty existence. In these there would be nothing but broken foundations, a few shallow holes where basements might have been or perhaps no trace of anything at all. This type of ghost may constitute a gratifying discovery for the man with a purely historical interest, who would feel a romantic reverence in saying: "The wonder of it! This is where the town of Galena used to be."

In the middle and largest group are the towns with a few or many of the old original buildings decaying, leaning or still stubbornly upright. Such a town, ghostly in the sense that it is a "shadowy substance of its former self", is not absolutely deserted. A building with any kind of roof is going to serve as shelter for some wandering sheepherder or prospector for a night or two or until he feels the urge to move on. A reasonably substantial house may still serve as home to some long time resident unwilling to give up the idea that the old place will bloom again. He may be living on a pension or simply not able to afford anything better. In towns like this will often be found some small business, if not too far off the beaten track — some little store, gas station or more likely, a tavern.

In the barely alive group the photographer will find his best hunting. Ignoring the television aerial on the little sod house or shanty, he will search out the relics best representing the long-departed, roistering days. Since the avowed purpose of this photographer is the recording of as many reminders of those days as possible, he will also set up his cameras in the third group which may be interpreted as ghost towns in varying degrees.

These places have never actually breathed their last or having taken a few labored gasps, have been resuscitated by some stimulant like the rise in the price of ore still available there. This is happening in many an old silver camp having all the characteristics of a ghost town. Or some of these old camps may be receiving the breath of life from the very tourists who insist they are ghost towns. Untold thousands have visited historic Virginia City, Nevada, its main street being thronged all summer. Many of these people spend most of their time in bars but yet they like to feel the place is a ghost town, as in a sense it is when its once vast extent and huge population is considered.

The true ghost town hunter is always looking for an ideal find, always hoping the next bend in the road will reveal the clutter that suits his romantic visions. In his fancy the road will turn into a weed-grown track swept by the restless wind and lined with false-fronted store buildings. Front doors will be hanging by single hinges and glassless windows will stare vacantly. There will be a complete array of furniture inside just as tenants left it. A heavy coating of dust will cover everything and this lucky discoverer will even consider the pack rat droppings on the plank floor as a bonus. Tatters of fancy wallpaper, imported from England, will flutter eerily to put a sound to loneliness. On the side of some hill there will be an old burying ground and inside the rickety fence board and marble monuments will mark the resting places of those who lived, loved and perhaps fought in the sagebrush.

Such old deserted towns grow fewer each year, their disappearance hastened by an insidious process of attrition. This is accomplished by visitors who take what they want as their just due for all the trouble getting there. Beautiful old brick buildings melt away, piece by piece, as souvenirs are carried off. A Victorian frame building loses its ginger-bread and Mexican adobe its twisted iron grills.

Beyond this, calculated destruction is a modern menace, carried on by a new horde of "treasure hunters" equipped with efficient metal detectors. The instruments are sold complete with directions for finding logical places that may contain long forgotten caches. "Pass the plate over all walls. There may be a treasure concealed between them." A flicker of the needle activated by some spike or insignificant piece of metal results in a wanton destruction of the wall and nothing found. Next winter the weakened building may collapse under the weight of snow.

Fortunately such acts of destruction, innocent or designed, are being slowed by law. When the perpetrators are discovered they are prosecuted. Several graves were opened in the old camp of Tumco, California, and bones removed. Those guilty were caught and punished. Antique bottle hunters did much damage in the nearly vanished town of Contention City in southern Arizona by excavating streets and floors. They were caught in nearby Tombstone and hailed into court. Most states now have laws protecting any kind of artifacts such as Indian relics or significant fossil remains and to prevent demolition of property. However this does not cover ghost towns on private lands. If posted against trespassing, such signs are to be respected. If the owner can be located he will most often give permission to explore.

We are often asked: "What are the most satisfying ghost towns you have ever found?" It's a difficult question to answer, having covered some 375 old camps of every description. Pinned down to specifics, it would be Elkhorn and Castle City, both in Montana, and Cascade Springs, South Dakota. Idaho's Silver City is superb and well known. Leesburg, almost inaccessible, is full of old log buildings rapidly falling into decay. Mogollon, New Mexico, is also hard to reach but very satisfying.

Every western state has many good examples as do most Canadian provinces and territories. The list could be extended to many states not western, notably the old copper towns of Michigan's Keweenaw Peninsula, jutting into Lake Superior, which was brought to our attention by Leighton George of the CUMBERLAND ADVOCATE in Cumberland, Wisconsin. The field grows ever larger.

There are a few points connected with the fascinating hobby of searching out the old camps that might be stressed, even though mentioned in former volumes of this series. Be equipped to camp as motels are not always handy in the more remote areas. Always make local inquiry when you come to a questionable dirt road as it may, and often does, get worse. And be prepared to hike when the road is impassable. If you take photographs, the use of a tripod, filters and a good light meter will reward you in better definition and exposure. Good hunting!

OLD PALACE BAKERY, dating from frenzied days of stampede to Yukon gold fields, still stands facing Klondike River near its junction with larger Yukon. When proprietor Charles F. Burkhard had only single building in center he loaded day's baking in push cart and peddled it in churning streets of Dawson City. Prosperity enabled him to add wing at left, shelter for new horse and wagon at right. This is the kind of building the ghost town hunter sees in his fondest dreams of conquest.

TABLE OF CONTENTS

Aurora, Nevada 60

Bennett, B. C. 113

Berlin, Nevada 52

Broken Hills, Nevada 72

Buena Vista, Colorado 186

Bumble Bee, Arizona 96

Chitwood, Oregon 156

Cleator, Arizona 88

Corrine, Utah 98

Crown King, Arizona 91

Dawson City, Y. T. 122

Douglas City, California 30

Elk City, Oregon 162

Galena, South Dakota 19

Glencoe, Wyoming 166

Grantsville, Nevada 49

Home, Washington 145

Ione, Nevada 44

Kernville, Oregon 163

Kings Valley, Oregon 150

McCabe, Arizona 84

Opal, Wyoming 169

Poncha Springs, Colorado   182

Pony, Montana   172

Port Blakely, Washington   140

Port Gamble, Washington   137

Port Ludlow, Washington   133

Rawhide, Nevada   66

Rochford, South Dakota   14

Rockerville, South Dakota   17

Rockland, Nevada   56

Rush to the Klondike   103

Shakespeare, New Mexico   175

Shasta, California   25

Shavano, Colorado   184

Sheridan, South Dakota   11

Skagway, Alaska   105

Stanton, Arizona   77

Sutro, Nevada   36

Union, Nevada   52

Union, Washington   143

Weaver, Arizona   81

Weaverville, California   32

Whiskeytown, California   21

Whitehorse, Y.T.   118

Acknowledgements and Bibliography

My sincere thanks to the many individuals who have contributed their time and energy in securing data for this book. My gratitude to the State Historical Societies and Libraries for their help.

ARIZONA, *publication of the Arizona Pioneers' Association*

THE BONANZA TRAIL *by Muriel Sibell Wolle*

MONTANA PAY DIRT *by Muriel Sibell Wolle*

STAMPEDE TO TIMBERLINE *by Muriel Sibell Wolle*

GHOSTS OF THE GLORY TRAIL *by Nell Murbarger*

GHOSTS OF THE ADOBE WALLS *by Nell Murbarger*

NEVADA'S TURBULENT YESTERDAY *by Don Ashbaugh*

AMERICAN GUIDE SERIES, *compiled by Federal Writers' Project for each western state*

HISTORIC SPOTS IN CALIFORNIA *by Hoover, Rensch and Rensch*

THE GHOST TOWNS OF CALIFORNIA *by Remi Nadeau*

LOST MINES AND TREASURES *by Ruby El Hult*

KLONDIKE '98 *by Ethel Anderson Becker*

ADOLPH SUTRO *by Robert E. Stewart, Jr. and M. F. Stewart*

MINING FRONTIERS OF THE FAR WEST *by Rodman Wilson Paul*

THIS WAS SAWMILLING *by Ralph Andrews*

FISH AND SHIPS *by Ralph Andrews*

HOW, WHEN AND WHERE ON HOOD CANAL *by Helen McReavy Anderson*

THE SHAKESPEARE STORY *by F. Stanley*

OREGON GEOGRAPHIC NAMES *by Lewis McArthur*

HERE ROLLED THE COVERED WAGONS *by Albert and Jane Salisbury*

OLD FORTS OF THE NORTHWEST *by Herbert M. Hart*

THE LAST WILDERNESS *by Murray Morgan*

GHOSTS OF GOLCONDA, *Black Hills Historical Guide Book by S. Goodale Price*

MAGAZINES — *Arizona Highways, Desert, Sunset, New Mexico.*

SHERIDAN, SOUTH DAKOTA

The memory of Father John Peter De Smet is held inviolate by the people of South Dakota in much the same manner as another Dutchman, Father Knickerbocker is all but a patron saint of New York. De Smet was an American Jesuit missionary to the Indians of the Upper Missouri and because he carried a Bible instead of a gun and had no cheap whiskey to trade for skins worth fifty times as much, he was their friend.

To prove this, a Sioux chief gave Father John a handful of gold nuggets and expressed the hope he would say nothing as to where he got them lest the greedy white men overrun the tribe's hunting grounds. Somewhere along the line however there was a leak. The news got out and numerous parties got into the Black Hills in search of this rumored store of gold.

Possibly the first formal expedition was that of General W. S. Harney in 1855 who took his men on a scouting trip from Laramie. They penetrated as far as they dared, considering the prevailing Indian menace. They camped at the base of a high peak and next morning held a conference to decide whether or not to go on to Ft. Pierre or return to the home base. The decision was made to climb the peak, reconnoiter and then take another vote.

The ascent was fairly easy, a flag planted at the top and the occasion "celebrated with many bumpers of champagne", which might account for

the men's courage to go on to Pierre in a hurry. The peak climbed may or may not be the one later named for General Harney. It is 7,242 feet in elevation, the highest peak in the United States east of the Rockies.

About a year later Lieutenant G. K. Warren led a party to the edges of the Hills. It was officially labeled "for scientific purposes" but this may have been a cover phrase for the real purpose, prospecting for gold, a frequent abuse of privilege and frowned upon by the Army. Warren had barely entered the Hills when, according to his statement: "We met a party of Indians who made such an earnest remonstrance that I did not think it prudent for a scientific expedition to venture further in that direction." So they struck a sensible retreat and were luckier than the members of a later party who lost their lives to the Sioux in the same locality.

The first actual panning of gold in the Black Hills was at French Creek, the discovery made by Horatio N. Ross on July 25, 1874. The find set off a rush which the Indians or U.S. Army or anyone else could not stem. Millions in gold were eventually removed from the stream and huge amounts later from the hard rock mines, although Ross died a pauper.

French Creek saw the first real operations in the gold bearing gravels and the town of Custer was established there because the existing stockade offered a show of protection from the marauding Sioux. Actual safety did not exist as miners could accomplish little inside the barricade and every venture outside invited and often met disaster. In spite of this much gold was recovered from French Creek, the prospectors eventually extending their search to other streams. One of these adventurous souls was Andrew J. Williams who made a find on Spring Creek.

Williams must have been made of sterner stuff than his partners because they waited at French Creek while he did the actual prospecting. When he found pay dirt the others were willing enough to join him, after they went to buy provisions and supplies. They made every effort to keep their secret but on arrival at the new Spring Creek diggings they found most of the good ground already staked off. Immediately there was an Indian attack which the combined forces repulsed, the site of the first discovery was then named Stand Off.

The usual collection of tents grew rapidly around Stand Off Bar, to be gradually replaced by log cabins, then false-fronted frame buildings. The fact that few miners found less than $20 worth of gold dust in their pans per day caused the new settlement to be christened Golden City, a name soon changed to Sheridan in honor of the extremely popular Civil War hero General Phil. As Sheridan grew it became the county seat and the government established there the first Federal court west of the Missouri.

The roistering gold camp took on all appearances of a solid city but maintained guards at the rifle ports on all buildings facing the edge of town

OLD WAGON WHEELS are piled against blacksmith shop, spokes and rims rotting, tires coming loose. In old days tires were replaced by heating them, metal expanding enough to allow them to be slipped back on rims. Cooling metal tightened them securely.

as protection from the Indians. This did not stop the violence within however. Several murderous attacks of whites on whites were staged in the largest of Sheridan's several brothels. Few decent women lived in the lawless camp and they were sagely indoors at dusk.

For several years the town was an important stop on the Denver to Deadwood stage line. Every so often it became a military camp when the troops of General Crook put up there and luck came in for the red light girls.

As gold began to fade from the stream so did Sheridan. People moved away rapidly when one of the largest mining syndicates gave up and the county seat was moved to Rapid City. The coming of the railroad caused abandonment of the stage line which had been so important to the place and with this several hotels and red light houses closed.

By 1900 the old camp was virtually a ghost town, buildings falling into decay year by year. Then in 1938 the Civilian Conservation Corps started a dam across Spring Creek near the point where the first discoveries of gold were made. With the approach of World War II other government agencies took over and completed it. Water soon lapped about the relics remaining in the old gold camp and then covered them forty feet deep. Called Lake of the Pines until 1945, it was then named in honor of the town that lay on its bottom. Sheridan Lake is now a popular place for fishermen and campers most of whom know nothing of the historic town down where the bass and crappies swim.

OLD BLACKSMITH SHOP stood in town of Sheridan, was salvaged as waters from dam constructed by CCC boys began to surround it, and moved to nearby Rockerville. Everpresent Ponderosa pines stand in background, same species as giants in Central Oregon and Washington but growing on smaller scale here. Their dark color gives Hills somber look from distance, explaining name "Black".

ROCHFORD, SOUTH DAKOTA

A deer kicked three men into a gold mine. Figuratively this is true and not strange since burros, ground squirrels and other animals have done the same. About half the rich mining areas of the country seem to have been pointed out by animals. In the case of the deposits on Montezuma Hill a startled deer was flushed from cover and in springing to flight, scuffed dirt from a rock to expose a vein of gold in the quartz.

A trio of hunters from Deadwood — Richard B. Hughes, William Van Fleet and M. D. Rochford — were scouring the hills for game in August of 1876 when they scared up the deer. They reported their find but in a day when such discoveries were being made by the clock, this modest one caused little excitement. The cold autumn was at hand and investigation was delayed until spring. In March a number of locations were staked out along Rapid Creek and all the way up the steep slope of Montezuma Hill.

Rochford became a lively place of about a thousand people if prospectors in cabins on the outskirts were included. At night miners poured in from the several gulches—Moonshine, Gimlet, Irish — and although they relaxed from their hard labor in the mills and placers, there seems to be little evidence of much lawlessness or violence.

This may have been due in some measure to the refining influence of the town's most notable and aptly named resident, Mrs. Annie D. Tallent, an accomplished woman of her day. Frontier women seemed to be either self-effacing, domestic home bodies who dwelt in anonymity or the flamboyant, bedizened common women of the camps, but Annie Tallent was a beacon light. Respectable and home-loving, she had many diverse interests, one of them the recording of history as she saw it pass. She wrote the only early chronicle of the area, THE BLACK HILLS OR THE LAST HUNTING GROUNDS OF THE DAKOTAHS.

An interesting episode from the book concerns an interview with Wild Bill Hickok whom she encountered on the streets of Cheyenne in 1875. She quotes him as saying: " 'Madam, I hope you will pardon my seeming boldness but knowing that you have recently returned from the Black Hills I take the pleasure of asking a few questions as to the country as I expect to go there soon. My name is Hickok.' I bowed low in acknowledgment of this supposed honor but I must confess that his next announcement startled me. 'I am called Wild Bill and you have no doubt heard of me'. 'Yes,' I candidly answered, 'I have often heard of Wild Bill and his reputation, I have thought it is not all credible, but perhaps he is not as bad as he is painted.' 'Well, as to that,' he replied, 'I suppose I am called a red-handed murderer, which I deny. That I have killed men, I admit, but never except in absolute self-defense or in the performance of an official duty. I never in my life took a mean advantage of an enemy.'

" 'Yet understand,' he added with a dangerous gleam in his eye, 'I never yet allowed a man to get the drop on me, but perhaps I may yet die with

OLD TOWN PUMP stands in foreground. Irish Gulch Dance Hall has been repaired, was in use for a time then fell quiet again. Dr. Mason sits on porch waiting for light on assay office building, is surrounded as usual by all children in town.

HOME OF PIONEER BLACK HILLS HISTORIAN, Annie D. Tallent, standing on quiet street in Rochford. Spelling of name on sign varies from that usually accepted.

my boots on.' His face softened a little. Was this perhaps a premonition of the tragic fate awaiting him?"

In keeping with its comparative restraint in behavior, Rochford exhibited similar moderation in its yield of gold. Although several stamp mills were in operation during its best years, production was never spectacular. Ores were admittedly low grade, the best of it milled, the rest discarded. This practice was in direct contrast to the policy of some mill owners in Hill City who stubbornly fed every-

ROCHFORD JAIL gives evidence there were exceptions to town's vaunted propriety amounting to dullness. View is from inside roofless structure. Builders used whatever material was at hand.

STANDBY MINE AND MILL was largest operation by far in Rochford. California capitalists bought original lode for $125,000, developed properties in big way. Large residence for superintendents was built near mill, was called The Mansion, now in ruins. Rapid Creek in foreground had good flow all year, providing power for mill. Old timers say there is plenty of gold left in mine but present costs prohibit operation. Shafts and tunnels were kept timbered for many years in hope of renewal. Tailing dumps are seen at right.

thing from the mines into the mills and went broke as a consequence.

Rochford went its sedate way, prospering conservatively until about 1885 when creeping paralysis began to slow the activities of the two stamp mills, Evangeline in Irish Gulch and Minnesota on Silver Creek. The ore coming to them was the same steady low grade as before but now it lacked the occasional good streaks that made operation profitable. Since capital could not be interested, the mills closed and so did most of the doors in the camp.

ROCKERVILLE, SOUTH DAKOTA

Charley Spicer was a hard and determined worker in an effort that took hard and determined work. The first summer along Spring Creek he panned and panned until his back was cricked and had very little to show for it. The next summer he was at it again even when there was almost no water and panning could be done only in the pools, most of which had been worked over before.

After a particularly disheartening day Charley was so tired he fell asleep after a supper of soggy flapjacks and beans. In one vivid sequence of a restless dream he was walking along a dry part of the creek and coming to a likely looking spot, he began to dig. Soon he was down to gravel that showed plenty of the long sought yellow flakes. There seemed to be plenty of water too and after the first panning he had a handful of black sand mixed with half a pound of pure gold.

The vision remained after he awoke and after more flapjacks and beans he set off to find the "dream spot". Strangely he did come to a place resembling it and began to dig. Two feet down he turned up a nugget worth $38. Hurrying back to camp he had no trouble interesting several moneyed men in forming a company to develop the Charley Spicer claim. The first need was water, plentiful in the dream, some distance away in reality. Flumes were built at a cost of some $8,000 from a small stream higher up the mountain that ran all summer.

Rewards were satisfactory but not spectacular. By the time the men had worked a few weeks winter stopped operations. In the spring, when freshets washed flume and all improvements down the gulch, the venture came to a sudden end.

William Keeler had better luck in Spring Creek. He and his little burro were on their way to Hill City by a short cut. This was in December and he was forced into an early camp by a snowstorm. The next day he saw the stream running through the snow and dipped a few pans, getting some color of gold. When he could travel he got to his destination, had a drink or two to loosen his tongue and told his friends Bart Henderson and D. G. Stillman of his experiences.

This meant, as soon as the weather cleared, the gulch was filled with eager claimants. Almost all had brought rockers since they were far more efficient at separating gold from gravel than the hand method, even though clumsy to transport. They resembled child's cradles, were often so called,

SOME REMAINING BUILDINGS and ruins of old Rockerville have been restored to suggest hectic days. Melodramas are given in old Opera House and between acts villain in cape walks town sneering at tourists, is seen here leaning against post. Burro was troublesome when photographer sought close up, insisted on nuzzling him to show friendliness.

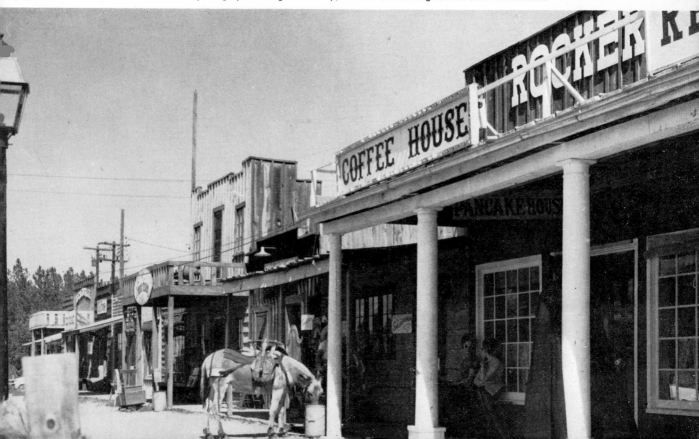

the box being a wooden trough, twenty inches wide by about forty long and four to twelve inches deep, the bottom a piece of sheet iron punched with holes a half-inch in diameter. Various substitutes were used for this bottom, even a mesh of small willow twigs with a canvas apron below them. Riffle bars about an inch thick were nailed to the bottom. An upright handle near the middle or at one end completed the arrangement.

If material to be washed was handy, one man could operate the contrivance, sitting on a rock or box and rocking it with one hand dipping water or gravel. Usually two men worked it, one rocking, the other shoveling. The gold was caught on the riffle bars, waste going out the lower end.

The abundant use of these "machines" was supposed to have given the gold camp the name of Rockerville. Actually, the area being very rocky, the first name was Rockville and altered by a contentious faction. An item in the BLACK HILLS JOURNAL of July 27, 1878, indicates that feelings ran high on this point. "There is a general desire in this place that the town shall be called in accordance with the post office designation—Rockville. The practice *must* be put in operation soon and now is as good a time as any to begin."

The gulch as a whole had a richness second only to Deadwood, the gold confined almost entirely to placers. Lawsuits, hassles over legal ownerships, often impeded operations as they did in other camps. One of the oldest stories in the Hills concerns a mine owner who was having trouble with the legal status of his property and sought the help of a miner to keep it in operation. The man replied: "I'm sorry I can't touch your vein. It's in litigation", to which the owner retorted with injured pride—

"You're a liar. It's in porphyry!"

Another incident said to have taken place in Rockerville involved a suit brought against a mine owner disputing his right to a location. The claim was paying richly but showed signs of petering out. The owner hired a lawyer who advised him to buy a supply of "Black Hills lightning" and keep the judge and jury drunk long enough to get out the rest of the best gold. By the time a delayed verdict was reached the mine was exhausted.

While rocker operations were carried on more easily in the spring much work was done in summer. Dirt could be trundled to rockers placed near any remaining pools of water. At the height of all these crude efforts, in and around 1880, the Black Hills Placer Mining Co. ran a flume to the placer beds from a dam above the town of Sheridan, fifteen miles away. A portable sawmill was put on skids, moved to flume line and advanced with the work, trees being cut down and made into lumber on the spot for flume and trestles.

The project was a big success for two years, its capacity load of 2000 miner's inches of water making possible the removal of $500,000 in gold. Other flumes were optimistically started, some finished were never used until the placers were exhausted and the few lodes pinched out.

Rockerville then became deserted and there came a time when the town could be described by pioneer Johnny Hunt in this way: "Rockerville was the prettiest little mining camp in the Black Hills with its rockers, puddle boxes, sluice boxes and quartz mills. The gulch was a solid mass of men and rockers, the side hills filled with houses and gopher holes where some found pockets of gold."

ROCKERS VARIED IN DETAIL from one model to another but all had same essentials. This one used perforated sheet iron seen at bottom of upper box.

GALENA, SOUTH DAKOTA

They came for gold and found silver. They came in March and needed secure shelter. They came from the prairies and knew how to build "soddies". So Galena had two booms — one in silver and one in hybrid sod houses.

The prospectors, coming in 1876, were the first men into Galena Creek and while they found a little gold, they knew silver was to be queen of the camp. They also knew they couldn't build sod houses as they had down on the flat lands. There they could cut root-bound, rectangular chunks of sod out of the ground and stack them into walls, roofing them with brush and dirt. Here in the mountains the dirt was loose and rocky so most miners made a compromise. They burrowed into banks far enough to create a small room, covering the front section with boughs and dirt. Galena soon presented a unique appearance among mining camps in the Black Hills with its double row of dugouts, one on each side of the Creek.

Henri Conzett however wanted a permanent house — and he wanted it right away, mining or no mining. A close friend of his had lost his top hair to Sioux marauders and Henri did not want this to happen to him. He would have a shelter that would serve as a fort in the event of an almost certain Indian attack. He managed to get the miners away from their diggings long enough to throw the fear of the redman into their hearts and get them to help him in his venture.

Each day Henri cut down several Ponderosa pines and stripped them of branches. At the end of the day three men were picked to help him haul the logs to the cabin site and place them on the others, then the helpers could go to their own dug-outs and cook supper.

When the walls were up more slender trees from the small stands of Lodgepole pines nearby were used as rafters and covered with the usual branches and dirt. When the cabin walls were chinked with clay, holes were left at strategic points for rifle ports. The dirt floor was made somewhat smooth, crude table, bunk and pot-bellied stove added and the residence-fort was ready for use — except for a door. Since there was no lumber to be had, one miner offered his idle sluice box. Henri knocked it apart, fashioned a stout door and hung it with wood and leather hinges.

By the time he was ready to get at his mining, Henri Conzett found all the good claims taken up and he had to be satisfied with one nobody wanted. The earliest good claims were the Florence and Sitting Bull, the better ones coming later — El Refugio, Gilt Edge, Merrit 1 and 2, Cora and Emmit. The Cora is still talked about as showing veins of pure silver.

Early operations in Galena were slow and somewhat futile, for lack of money. When such men as Robert Florman and Col. J. W. Davey stepped in and financed the mines, the camp boomed. By 1880 a twenty-stamp mill had been built to crush the

HOME OF MRS. CHARLES BENTLEY. Born in this house, her father managed Gilt Edge mine. Home now looks out on idyllic scene — trees, green hills, sparkling stream replacing hundreds of commercial and residence buildings. Tree in yard is second growth Douglas fir, quite common here although predominating trees are Ponderosa pines. Mrs. Bentley is fearful of intrusion, wishes no development of area, is suspicious of and unfriendly to strangers.

ever-mounting piles of gleaming ore from the Sitting Bull.

Typical of the day is an item from the BLACK HILLS TIMES of March 10, 1880: "A gentleman from Galena says people are wild with excitement over a new strike in the Cora mine . . . a piece of ore so lousy with silver that a piece of it when broken in two was again stuck together quite firmly by inserting the sharp protuberances of pure metal into the cavities of the rock from which they had been taken."

By 1882 the rows of dugouts had been replaced by false-front stores and hotels, flanked by a goodly number of houses. The 4th of July that year "was ushered in by the booming of giant powder which shook the buildings from roof to basement. The fronts of most of the buildings were shaded by graceful firs lending to our streets the appearance of comfort and grandeur. The patriotic ladies had previously prepared large quantities of cake, ice cream, fruits and other delicacies of which the great ugly male patriots partook freely and were made happy." At dusk there was a display of fireworks in front of Hadley's place, followed by a dance in the "superbly decorated" Brown's Hall where "the light fantastic was tripped far into the night."

While there seemed to be no clouds on the horizon at the time the celebration was to be one of the last in Galena. First sign of a coming catastrophe was the serving of an injunction on Col. Davey, who had blown in his smelter in 1880 and was following up the ledge on the dip "Beyond his sidelines" said the lawyers for the Richmond claim. The colonel was forced to close the properties while litigation was going on and every resident of Galena was on edge over this threatened end to the town's biggest source of income. Then Davey's son Frank and the watchman of the Sitting Bull, Billy Thatcher, got into an altercation with an employee of the contesting Richmond mine in a saloon which ended in a blaze of gunshot and the death of the Richmond man, one Patrick Gorman.

At the trial Thatcher claimed he fired in self defense, that Gorman had pulled a gun on him as soon as the quarrel started. He won acquittal on these grounds but Gorman had been well liked and Thatcher found it expedient to leave town. He did not come back.

Lengthy legal hassles over the Sitting Bull operations kept the mines closed and people began to be starved out. Davey himself left Galena to be followed by many others. The place reverted to the status of a ghost town until 1895 when silver experienced so high a rise in price several of the mines not involved in the litigations were reopened. Two years saw the end of this flurry and Galena lay back again.

Decay has taken almost all the buildings. The trees have grown up again, the stream runs clear and sparkling, uncontaminated by mill tailings. The site is as lovely for vacationers as if never spoiled by a roistering boom camp.

GALENA SCHOOL has been kept in repair since construction in 1882. Mrs. Bentley states her mother was first teacher, records listing first as Nellie Wynn who probably married later. Other early teachers were George McCune, Florence Ryan, Lulu Schall and Kitty Doyle. Long list of others followed in 71 years of school's service. Original virgin stand of typical Ponderosa pines was cut for town's sawmills, present luxurious stand all second growth.

WHISKEYTOWN, CALIFORNIA

A miner could do without tears. He wanted no part of them unless they were tears of joy at finding a rich pocket of gold. But when a mule fell off a rocky cliff and with the mule went two kegs of whiskey, slam-banging down the rocky slope to end up at the bottom smashed to smithereens, the precious liquid dissipated into a stream . . well what could a poor miner do but cry?

This is what happened in the mountains between Redding and the Pacific Ocean, in general the Trinity River country of northern California. And when one miner sobbed: "This is sure one hell of a whiskey creek now", the stream was called Whiskey Creek and the miners revered the memory of the lost hooch by naming the camp Whiskeytown.

Jedediah Strong Smith opened up the country in 1828 on an expedition to Oregon. After pushing up the Buenaventure River (now Sacramento) he found the rocky hills coming so close to the river it was impossible to travel, so moved due west and then north up the Coast. He thus penetrated the Trinity Alps and found the going hard, rocks in the river bed "mangling the horses' feet." Smith's name served as the river's for years and when it was changed to Trinity, "Smith" became the name for another in Del Norte County.

Forced to leave the comparatively easy grade of the cascading stream, Smith's party veered almost straight up the mountainside, scrambling through thick undergrowth. Topping the ridge the party crossed into Humboldt County and eventually met the ocean. Jedediah Smith had opened up a trail that was roughly the foundation of today's roads between the Sacramento Valley and the Coast. In his footsteps followed trappers of Hudson's Bay Company on their travels to and from Oregon. Prospectors also used the route and in 1848 gold in large quantities were found in the Trinity and its tributaries. Although one report had "nuggets lying around in the gravel like walnuts" there was no such rush here as in the Mother Lode. Yet several wildly roaring gold camps sprang up in the Trinity Alps and Whiskeytown was one of the roughest.

At first a nameless clutter of shacks and tents on an anonymous stream, they bred more and got a proper name when the mule toppled off the high trail and the train headed for Shasta City, a camp farther up the creek and noted for its colossal thirst, was short one keg of whiskey.

As Whiskeytown grew large enough to petition for a postoffice, officials scoffed at such a crude name and suggested Blair, which in turn was ridiculed by the miners as was Schilling and Stella. Although called all these names sedately, it was Whiskeytown to the men with the picks and shovels.

OLD ROCK JAIL in Whiskeytown was stoutly built but couldn't resist modern bulldozers which cleared ground to be covered by waters of new lake. Still standing when author-artist Muriel Sibell Wolle took this photo, it was gone in 1963.

It was womanless for years until, said a valley newspaper of 1852: "Whiskeytown's first white woman has taken up her residence there", leaving the reader to guess her purpose. Later that year the paper reported one of the town's several bartenders was "insulted" by a fellow citizen and ventilated him with two bullet holes. The victim had many friends and with a rope over a tree branch they fixed the bartender so he could shoot no more of them.

Late in the '50s a man named Bon Mix erected "a commodious hotel" which embraced a fine saloon and dance hall. The girls employed there were described as "young ladies of probable virtue" but at the edge of town in a small row of cribs were several other ladies whose virtue was highly improbable.

Besides washing the gravel of Whiskey Creek, miners were working small hard rock mines, of a type known as "gopher holes." A man would start a horizontal tunnel, working in a prone position, enlarging the hole barely enough to crawl forward. He had just enough head room to hack at the rock and heap the chippings in a gunnysack ahead of him. When the bag was full he wriggled out hind-blind and dumped out the loose rock. There is no record of any of these burrowings paying off much, certain-

22

ly not enough for the hazard involved. Falling rock could have crushed a man or blocked off his exit.

Official records, always far below actual figures because of "bootlegging", showed $25 million was recovered from the gulches around Whiskeytown. Many other ghostly camps have a few stubborn inhabitants who stoutly maintain that the old place will boom again when the price of gold rises, there being plenty of the yellow stuff around. Not so in the case of Whiskeytown. Two hundred feet of cold mountain water covers the site.

The Bureau of Reclamation has diverted the waters of the Trinity River over twenty miles into the Sacramento by way of the newly created Whiskeytown Lake, formed by the dam of the same name, which was dedicated by President Kennedy in September, 1963, as one of his last official acts. High above, on dry land, a "new" postoffice, built of lumber salvaged from an old saloon in the original town, is plainly marked "Whiskeytown." No one argues about the name now.

RUSTY SKIP BUCKET was safely removed to level above rising waters, still lying in clutter of saloon lumber and other salvaged materials. Heavy container was used to remove ore from mine shaft, raised and lowered by ropes over windlass. When rope became frayed, miners stood clear of load.

FRENCH GULCH near Whiskeytown once boasted street lined solidly with false front buildings. The few remaining are defaced by posters in front, show atmosphere and age in rear. At left is stone structure serving as bank, other was store with living quarters on upper story. Backyard fence is smothered with ancient grapevines, leafless here in March. First discoveries were made and mining done by Frenchmen in 1849. Later main workings were operated by Washington Quartz Mining Company. When rich veins were discovered in 1852, Shasta **Courier** reported: "Such rich diggings have been struck that miners are tearing down their houses to pursue the leads which run under them."

SHASTA, CALIFORNIA

Dick Barter might have lived out his life as an honest citizen but the cards were stacked against him. He arrived in California from Canada just too late to share in the first big bonanzas of the Sierra gold rush. His claim was on Rattlesnake Bar, near Auburn, and when he got there with a sister and cousin he found the gravels already depleted. Discouraged, his relatives went north to settle on a homestead at Sweet Home, Oregon.

But Dick stayed on, persistently working his claim. Never admitting its thin yield, he bragged about it so noisily in the Auburn saloons he was soon called "Rattlesnake Dick". If the nickname didn't force him into crime it at least made the rumors about his shady conduct easy to believe.

The first of these came about when a miner, who had taken a dislike to Dick's loud talk, reported he had seen the Canadian stealing from a little store near his claim. Dick was arrested, tried and acquitted, but the seed of suspicion was planted.

Next a Mormon named Crow missed his mule and brought charges of theft against Dick, even stating he had seen the accused taking the animal. This evidence was enough to convict the hapless man but before sentence was passed (which could have been death by hanging) the real culprit turned up, a man resembling Barter.

But now he was a marked man and it seemed to Dick that everyone looked at him with an accusing eye. Completely discouraged with his claim, he left

the area for a mining town farther north — Shasta. It was enough removed, he thought, so he could start life again without the hated nickname and its sinister influence. Soon after arrival in the booming camp at the edge of the Trinity Alps he found work to his liking and settled down to what he hoped would be a peaceful existence.

He had two good years before some men from Auburn came to town and spotted him. In no time the information got around that "this man is Rattlesnake Dick, a fugitive from Auburn where he's been in all kinds of scrapes." And now he was looked at sidewise in Shasta. He was later quoted as saying: "I can stand it no longer. I have been driven to a hereafter. Now my hand is against everyone's as everyone's is against me."

Dick Barter lost no time in getting into his new way of life, holding up a man for enough to pay his way back to Auburn and more familiar territory. In best dime novel tradition, he "signed" his first dishonest deed, telling his victim: "If anyone asks who robbed you, tell them Rattlesnake Dick, the Pirate of the Placers".

For the first year or so his crimes were for chicken feed but he was laying plans to intercept a big shipment of gold that would come along the road through Shasta. The bullion would be sent south from Yreka by mules branded with the name of their owner, Wells Fargo. Therefore it would be necessary to transfer the gold to unmarked animals

OLD SKETCH SHOWS SHASTA before fire of June 14, 1853, which destroyed almost entire town in thirty minutes. Adams Express offices, Old Dominion and St. Charles Hotels, largest in town, shown here, were rebuilt within four years as solid brick, fireproof structures.

"TREES OF HEAVEN", grown from seeds brought home by nostalgic Chinese miners, are common sights in most milder climate mining camps. Photo shows bare limbs of early March outlined by low-angled sunlight.

immediately after the holdup. Dick knew where to steal the fresh mules and he would do this part of the job himself. George Skinner would be head of the gang performing the holdup, George's brother Cyrus helping gather up the new mules.

The robbery was committed without a hitch although the train was accompanied by twenty armed guards. George Skinner had only six men but the element of surprise helped him subdue the guards. They were tied to trees as Skinner's men made off with the loaded mules.

Arriving at the rendezvous site above Shasta, the high-spirited highwaymen waited for Rattlesnake Dick and his string of fresh mules. After several days of worry about Dick's absence and the possibility of a misunderstanding about the meeting place, Skinner and his boys were as jumpy as fleas. Expecting a posse from Shasta anytime, scouts combed the gulches and sentries kept constant

watch. In desperation a decision was made to make tracks with half the gold. The $80,000 in bullion represented far too much weight to carry without mules but, Skinner said, they could manage half of it and he would bury the other half alone. As he moved half the gold, a Mexican started to follow him and was shot on the spot. With part of the treasure buried, the gang headed for their hideout near Folsom, south of the American River.

They got there at night and buried the second half of the bullion, then started for Auburn to find out what had detained Dick. The fact was, the Auburn jail was detaining him now for he had been caught stealing the mules — but George Skinner would never know it. At Shasta, Wells Fargo detective Jack Barkley had deduced the job had been handled by Rattlesnake Dick's gang and knowing the location of the hideout, he took his posse in that direction. The two parties met in the moonlight on

Trinitys to the west and Oregon to the north de-the Folsom-Auburn road and the first shot Barkley fired killed Skinner. Four men deserted the posse but the rest subdued the robber gang and brought them into Auburn. One of them, Bill Carter, received a pardon for revealing where the second half of the gold was concealed. With George Skinner dead, the first half was unrecoverable. The $40,000 in bullion remains hidden near Shasta to be added to the several other celebrated stories of hidden treasure in California.

Rattlesnake Dick broke out of the Auburn jail and made a brief return to his chosen career. One night, after a holdup, he was shot to death by a pursuing posse. On his body was found a pathetic letter from his sister, imploring her errant brother to give up his life of crime and join her on the farm.

While all this was going on, Shasta was not too much perturbed. The town was full of rough characters and accustomed to events of this sort. Stringing up her own horse thieves and holdup men from the gallows at the rear of the courthouse, she was not too much bothered by crimes outside of town.

LONG ROW OF FADING BRICK REMNANTS mark outlines of Shasta's once teeming business section. Most buildings retain fragments of iron doors and shutters commonly used, intended to keep burglars and fire out, or contain fires starting within.

STEEP BANK behind brick structures causes heavy runoff in rainy periods, while several semi-permanent springs flow most of year. Provision was made for drainage by bricked gutters between buildings. Here, in early March, rivulet is conducted to street as in 1850s.

Shasta was little more to start with than a camp at the gateway to the rich mines in the back country, a stage stop between the level valleys of the Sacramento and the snowy peaks of the Trinitys, the head of "Whoa Navigation" in the vernacular of the day.

Originally called "Reading's Springs" by the first settlers who arrived at the site shortly after Major Pierson Reading found fifty ounces of gold a day nearby, the name was changed to Shasta next year. The mountain for which it is named is not far to the north, is a magnificent old volcano of more than 14,000 feet in elevation, covered with spectacular glaciers on the north and east sides. At its foot is the present day town of Mount Shasta, not to be confused with the roistering old Shasta above Redding.

A hundred mule trains and teams were known to stop in Shasta on a single night. Its strategic position caused a fast growth of outfitters and suppliers. Mule trains heading for the mines in the

REAR OF OLD COURTHOUSE in Shasta shows jail on first floor, gallows on level with courtroom. First legal hanging here was that of a man named Higgins on November 10, 1855. Last of long succession was John Baker on August 24, 1874. Baker was one of pair guilty of holdup and murder. His companion, Charles Crouch, wanted execution over quickly but Baker stalled death for a few minutes by request that he be allowed to sing a song remembered from his childhood. It was granted and he sang "Faded Flowers", the last two stanzas being:

Oh! how dark looks this world and
    how dreary
When we part from the ones that
    we love;
But there's rest for the faint and
    the weary
And friends meet with loved ones
    above!

And in Heaven I can but remember
When from earth my proud soul
    shall be free
That no cold chilly winds of December
Can take my companions from me.

layed obtaining full supplies until arrival in Shasta. One of the largest supply houses was that of Bull, Baker and Co. The firm erected a substantial brick building in 1853 replacing a wooden one destroyed by fire. The structure still stands today, a unit in the highly publicized, at that time, "longest row of brick buildings in California." The story is told of one of the Bull, Baker principals being stopped by a mule team owner on his way to breakfast. The latter was anxious to be on his way, joined the trader at breakfast and bought $3,000 worth of goods before the ham and eggs got to the table.

Shasta kept her position of shipping center until 1872 when the California and Oregon Railroad reached the six-mile distant city of Redding in the valley. This was a severe blow and when the neighboring placers became exhausted in 1888, the fading city lost county seat honors and quietly died.

MASONIC HALL shows through gaping doorway. Lodge building has been well cared for, is still in use. Treasured in vault is first charter of Western Star Lodge No. 2 which was brought from Missouri by Peter Lassen. He carried precious document in metal cylinder for protection against fire or water. Lassen made trip by ox train, became well known figure all over northern California, numerous prominent features including Lassen Peak being named for him.

DOUGLAS CITY, CALIFORNIA

When Anderson's riderless mule returned, the settlers knew the Indians had taken him. Constantly harassed by them, the white men were surprised Andy had gone out to the range alone. A search party was formed and sure enough, there was the body, riddled with arrow wounds and no sign of the cattle. There was only one thing to do — find those murderous Indians and kill the lot of them.

The party split in half, the first group trailing the Indians to their camp, near where Douglas City was later settled. The second group rounded up more men, seventy strong and bent on revenge, and caught up with the first bunch of whites. Taken by surprise, almost the entire Indian village of over a hundred and fifty braves, squaws and children was wiped out, even to the few who escaped into Bridge Gulch.

There were three exceptions — two little girls and a boy. The girls were found by a man sickened by all the slaughter. He protected them and, one, Ellen Clifford, lived at Weaverville for many years. The other was cared for by a woman whose ideas of charity were warped as she sold the girl to a teamster for $45. The boy lay hidden behind a log and waiting until it was safe, made his way to another Indian camp. Years later, as "Indian Bob", he turned up in Douglas City and told his story.

The history of Douglas City is closely related to that of Major Pierson Reading. He had a part in the Bear Flag Revolt at Sonoma in 1846, later joined Fremont's battalion and finally returned to his ranch four miles east of Cottonwood, between Red Bluff and Redding.

When the big news about the discovery of gold at Coloma broke, Major Reading hurried there to see what the truth was. He found a seething mass of humanity well on its way to start the biggest gold rush ever known, but he himself was too late to find a good claim there. He reasoned that if there was gold in the American River, there must also be gold in the Trinity. He was familiar with that stream through the Trinity Alps, the rugged range of snowy mountains northwest of his ranch. He knew it as Smith River and later renamed it Trinity under the misapprehension that it flowed into Trinidad Bay as noted on old Spanish charts.

In 1858 Major Reading related how very right he had been in deducing there must be gold nearer home, obtainable without the heavy competition in the Sierra. "In the month of July, 1848," he recalled, "I crossed the mountains of the coast range at the head of Middle Cottonwood Creek and struck the Trinity at what is now called Reading's Bar; prospected for two days and found the bars rich in gold; returned to my home in Cottonwood and fitted out an expedition for mining purposes; crossed the mountains where the travel passed about two years ago from Shasta to Weaver.

"My party consisted of three white men, one Delaware, one Chinook and sixty Indians from the Sacramento Valley. With this force I worked the bar bearing my name. I had with me a hundred head of cattle and an abundant supply of other provisions. After about six weeks of work, parties came in from Oregon who at once protested about my Indian labor. I then left the stream and returned to my home where I have since remained in the enjoyment of the tranquil life of the farmer." The major might have added the $80,000 in gold he had extracted from the bar helped him enjoy it.

Lost are the names of the Oregon men who interrupted the major's efforts but Reading's Bar is located on the Trinity River immediately below the Douglas City bridge. More and more Oregon men came to mine the area until it became necessary to build a crude, high-altitude road over the pass to Yreka. The road, nearly impassable at best, became completely so after every heavy snowstorm. The solution to this problem was to drive a herd of oxen to the summit, keep them handy there, and after each storm let them trample the loose snow to firm footing.

During 1850 an even greater number of gold seekers came into the country by way of San Francisco, where they boarded ships for the voyage north to make perilous landings in Trinidad Bay, thence by small boats part way up the Klamath to the point where the Trinity enters that river, then on foot to the diggings. By the end of the next year every stream and mountain pocket had been explored and prospected, and by the end of 1852 the Trinity River, wrapped in solitude only a short time before, was solidly lined with toiling miners, sluices and rockers from Salyer to Garville.

OLD WATER TOWER — only remains of Douglas City, just above site of Major Pierson Reading's epochal discovery of gold along Trinity River. Lower part of tower served as living quarters until recent years. Guardian tree is Ponderosa pine, often called "yellow pine". These timber trees, together with sugar pines — similar in appearance but with very long cones — and Douglas firs, constitute most of the forest cover in the Trinity Alps at this altitude, 1700 feet.

WEAVERVILLE, CALIFORNIA

Weaverville is a lively wraith now, ghostly only in that it is filled with relics and mementos of its boisterous past . . . of a time when board walks rattled with the clomp of miners' boots . . . when the streets were filled with Chinamen screaming in a tong war . . . of a period when newspapers could report on a Tuesday — "Sunday two persons were killed, yesterday buried and today almost forgotten."

In two blocks on both sides of the street the business section of Weaverville's Chinatown was crammed with 2,500 Chinese. Laundries, joss houses, gambling cribs and opium dens had oriental fronts and when the dives offered more for the customer than the white joints and cut into their profits, there was trouble. The Chinese lived anywhere — in warrens, back rooms of stores or in hovels on the fringes of town.

Most of them came from Canton or Hong Kong and the rival tongs under the two allegiances, were bitter enemies. Hatred built up until something had to give and a battle fought. In 1854 a day was set for it — July 4, popular in Weaverville for hangings, picnics, sporting events and now war.

Preparations went on for weeks, blacksmiths fashioning mining tools into cudgels and tridents, the latter favorite among feuding orientals since pitchforks were not available and guns strictly forbidden to Chinese.

On the appointed day rival forces of some six hundred Chinese gathered on a field above Five Cent Gulch, a mile east of town. Weapons flew and blood flowed until the up-to-now amused white spectators stepped in and stopped the mayhem.

Eight Chinese and one American were killed, many wounded and carried off the flat and a dozen or two with minor injuries limped home. Newspapers next day reprimanded the whites for allowing the bloody scrap but were tacitly reminded that they had encouraged it as a "coming attraction", and as one American defended himself: "We thought it was to be sort of a comic opera." Five Cent Gulch and the flat above it was shortly found to be rich in gold and was deeply mined.

It was in 1850 that John Weaver of Mississippi arrived in the locality, one of the wildest and most remote in California. Nothing disturbed the silence but an occasional scream of a mountain lion or the rushing sounds of the rivers. John (some say William) Weaver found gold to the extent of about $15 a day. The news got out and soon a village of log houses had sprung up. Steady growth was at first slow, so inaccessible was the gold field. Whichever

HANDSOME COURTHOUSE has been in constant use since construction in early days. Kept in good repair (note stucco over bricks), offices modernized but atmosphere of mid-nineteenth century is retained.

GRACEFUL SPIRAL STAIRCASES are unique feature of Weaverville's main street. Greatest building period was in 1850s when, as many wooden structures burned, solid brick ones replaced them. Many had offices and stores on second floors with balconies reached by outside, private stairways. Metal work was done in local blacksmith shops. Original iron doors are still in use upstairs in some buildings.

on dwindling reserves went sky-high. When the thaws finally did come and trains began arriving, morale had reached a miserable low. It was bad enough to have food stocks reduced to a little grain but the horrible catastrophe was — only a few gallons of whiskey left in the last keg.

Violence flared in Weaverville, with comic opera aspects along with grim results. There was the incident of the traveling man in the pig sty. He had arrived from Klamath in the morning, made calls on several prospects and had his pockets well lined by evening. This called for a celebration and he led the town on a round of the saloons. By midnight, thoroughly drunk, he groveled around for a place to sleep and settled for a cozy pig pen.

The drummer was still there in the morning but what had been in his pockets wasn't. He protested loudly that he'd been robbed and Weaverville's scapegoat, one Seymour, was brought to the sheriff for questioning. On previous occasions, when he had suddenly "come into money", he had headed for the closest bar. This time he had not. He was cold sober and had no money on him. Highly offended Seymour asked: "Why don't you look in the straw in that pig mud?" Sure enough, there was the missing cash. The weekly newspaper had some unsympathetic comments: "The money was found in the hog pen where the sot had found shelter and suitable companionship."

Not so funny was the fate of John Fehly, who also owed his troubles to the bottle. Stoned to the gills, he lunged from the Diana Saloon one day, shooting wildly in every direction. A random bullet caught well-liked Dennis Murray in the head and killed him. Fehly was seized by Dennis' friends and forced to jail. They all had lynch fever but Fehly had sobered up and was not about to let a noose be twisted around his neck without a struggle. He gave it but the hanging committee called for "The Infant", a gangling young giant, six feet six, and used to putting down insurgents. He threw a hammerlock around Fehly and jerked until the murderer gave

way the eager argonaut chose to get there he was up against hardships. Especially bad was the route from San Francisco by sailing vessel to Trinidad and the trip up the inner valleys by ox and wagon train, with Digger Indians always a menace. Yet Weaverville did grow and became the county seat of Trinity County very early — a dubious honor since she had no competition.

The Trinity Alps are often compared to the High Sierra but the differences are great. The latter range is strung out lengthwise, the Trinity mountains are bunched. Sierra altitudes reach far above 14,000 feet while most Trinity peaks are between 8,000 and 9,000 feet. The latter group is near the ocean and moisture laden storms pile up snow to depths unknown in the Sierra.

These snows made plenty of trouble for the first miners who were unprepared for them. The winter of 1852-53 was especially severe and flimsy-roofed cabins were crushed beneath the weight. Several homes back against the bases of steep slopes were smothered by avalanches, the slides most prevalent towards spring. To make matters worse, incoming mule trains carrying food and candles for lighting etc. were unable to get through the drifts and prices up. "All right, you!" he panted. "At least put a coal in my pipe." Someone lit the pipe, the noose slipped over it and the trap sprung.

Weaverville got along without a jail for some years by the expedient of quick execution or release. "A man is either guilty or not guilty", the people said. But eventually the decision took longer and a wooden jail was built which was soon set on fire by a prisoner smoking in his bunk. A strong, fireproof one was built of brick and this set the trend for a change in the general aspect of the town, wood giving way to brick as fire forced the issue. Even before the town was changed, it had some 2,000 people and to serve them were fourteen saloons, four hotels, many stores, the inevitable gambling houses and girl joints.

There was wild jubilation in Weaverville in 1858 when the wagon road came through to Shasta which connected the town to the outside world. Commented the weekly TRINITY JOURNAL, started two years before: "Weaverville now assumes its proper place among the foremost cities of our fair state of California. The opening of the luxurious new wagon road ends our condition of isolation."

PLAINLY VISIBLE from State Highway 299 are evidences of huge devastation wrought by one of the largest hydraulic operations in world. Baron Le Grange mine, opened in 1851, directed powerful streams of water at slopes of Oregon Gulch Mountain, washing away tons of soil, running mud into sluice boxes where heavy gold settled to bottom, caught on slat ridges, was recovered in periodic "clean up". Mud flowed on downstream to spread over farm lands, ruining them. Destruction became widespread in valleys, finally resulted in federal Anti-Debris or Sawyer Act of 1883, putting end to all hydraulic operations. Later, restrictions were eased under certain conditions.

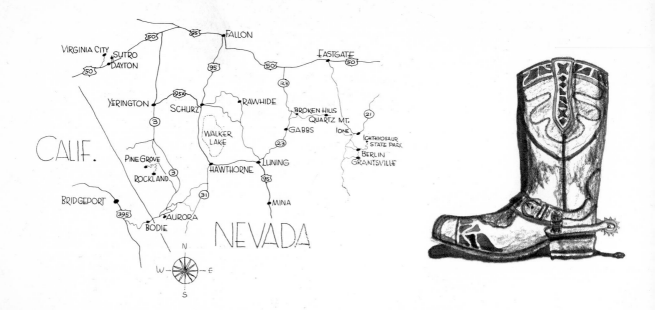

SUTRO, NEVADA

Sweet are the uses of adversity. Every time a man was killed in the building of the Sutro Tunnel in the 1870s, the other men used it as an excuse for a big time. After the funeral and burial at the cemetery in Virginia City, they hung on a big drinking party and then needed two more days to sober up.

The big hitch in this giddy round was Adolph Sutro. He wanted no delays in the building of this tunnel and did not see why the dead could not be buried right in the new town of Sutro at the mouth of the tunnel. He laid out a burial ground but the men quickly told him it wouldn't work. When a premature blast killed Kelly, they said the burial would be at Virginia City, same as usual: "Because Kelly will be lonely all by himself in that new ground."

Sutro had to swallow one more lay off but shortly a careless powder man left some loose blasting material near a battery. A spark caught it and the explosion killed two men. "Now," said Adolph Sutro in Prussian gutteral, we have the funeral here and start new cemetery." Aching for another bust, the men searched frantically for some next-of-kin to insist on carrying out the final rites on Mt. Davidson. Finding none they were forced to have the services at Sutro and get back to work the next morning.

The story of the ghost town of Sutro is the story of Adolph Sutro. It begins in Aachen (Aix-la-Chapelle) Prussia, when on April 29, 1830, Adolph Heinrich Joseph Sutro was born. One of eleven children whose father Emanuel, and uncle Simon, owned a large woollen factory. Young Adolph had many interests, in machines at the mill, exploring the heavens at night with his telescope and in botany through his many walks at the edge of town. Adolph loved books too and acquired a knowledge of general science far beyond that of his brothers which furnished a grounding for his later interest in California and Nevada mining that led to the building of the tunnel to the Comstock Lode.

In 1848 his father went on a business trip carrying a brace of pistols for protection against bandits. On the way home, not having occasion to use them, he discharged the loads in the air. The horses bolted, throwing him out of the carriage and Emanuel suffered a broken back which paralyzed him. During the year he lived, the family's funds were nearly exhausted and Adolph was compelled to leave school at sixteen.

In 1850 the young man made his big move to America. In New York he was almost immediately caught up in the California gold fever and in two weeks left for San Francisco. His crossing of the

THIS WAS CENTER OF SUTRO. At left is blacksmith shop, complete with forge, in front of it ore car on tracks which lead from mouth of tunnel at left, out of picture. At right is large warehouse. Townsite was surveyed in 1872 in neat gridiron pattern. Streets were 80 feet wide with exception of central one leading from tunnel, 200 feet wide and called Tunnel Avenue. Lots cost $500 up. Cottonwood trees may be descendants of those originally planted along avenue although Sutro preferred more exotic types some of which could not survive climate. Each lot purchaser was required to plant at least one tree and care for it.

Isthmus was the usual battle of mosquitoes, thieving natives in the guise of guides and narrow escapes from dysentery, cholera and smallpox. At Panama City he was lucky in being booked for passage to California in a week where others were held for many.

In San Francisco, where one day he would be its first citizen, he was just another foreigner. Almost starving by the time his trunks arrived, he started at once selling the German cloth and articles they contained. When he had enough money for a few meals and a ticket to Stockton where a cousin

lived, the two set up a store on the levee. He stayed with this a year or so, then returned to San Francisco with enough of a stake to start a tobacco shop and two stores. One was a supply house from which he shipped groceries and mining equipment to the Mother Lode by way of Stockton and to the Northern Mines through Sacramento. When the Trinity Mountain area was opened up at Weaverville and Shasta, Sutro shipped by water up the Sacramento River to Redding, thence to the mines by mule-back, or up the Coast to Trinidad Bay where the goods were transferred to small boats on the Klam-

STRING OF ORE CARS still on tracks in middle of Tunnel Avenue. At first cars were drawn by mules, later by small electric engines.

ath River, then in turn to mules for the rest of the way along the Trinity River trail.

Then he made a false move. A year or two later when the gold rush to the Fraser River was in full swing, Adolph left his wife and two children to go north and start a cigar store in Victoria. But the first full migration was over and depression was setting in. He returned to San Francisco to hear of the new gold push to Washoe in Nevada.

He went there, to Mt. Davidson and worked out a new system of greater efficiency for recovery of gold and silver from quartz, not only from virgin ore but in old dump residue. So he settled down at Dayton, at the foot of the mountain, and organized a company, built mills with stamps and roasting ovens and was soon making $10,000 a month.

As soon as the mill was well established he sent for his brother Hugo to run it. For some time there had been a plan in Adolph's head, a plan which was to embrace every thought he had for many years. It was to build a tunnel, a horizontal bore several miles long to start at a level lower than the bottoms

of the deep shafts descending from Virginia City. Those mine shafts were suffering badly from poor ventilation, even with forced air. Temperatures in the depths were so high that water, in itself an ever increasing menace, turned to steam and the high humidity suffocated the already exhausted miners. Sutro reasoned that such an opening to the outside air would drain off the water, ventilate the mines and bring temperatures down. It would also provide a cheap exit for Comstock ores.

With Hugo to take care of things at the mills, Sutro traveled all over the area by horseback, seeking out a logical spot for starting such a tunnel. As a skilled amateur surveyor, he actually lined up the nearly nine-mile tunnel to connect with the bottom of the Savage mine shaft so accurately that 13 years later, when the last charge of powder was set off, it caved in a hole in the side of the shaft.

The hard part was raising the money. Adolph Sutro would never have imagined anyone would stand in the way of such a humanitarian project, one that would benefit everyone, but he proved to be less a logician than he was engineer. He pointed out

38

that with the tunnel completed, the necessity for Virginia City would be eliminated, that all mills and operations would then move to his new town to be named Sutro, where all mining operations and ore refining could be carried out on a level with the present operations.

The interests controlling the wealth of Virginia City would listen to no talk of this kind. The most formidable foe of Sutro and his plan was the Bank of California. It had already foreclosed on a number of Comstock mines, where poor management and less-rich ores had forced insolvency, and it owned many huge mills not only at Virginia City but on down the grade at Silver City and Gold Hill. Furthermore it was planning to build a railway to the city on top of the mountain for prospective patrons of the banks, hotels and restaurants and to haul practically all equipment and supplies to the mines — a veritable monopoly with the wagon roads so steep and rough. If Sutro's tunnel was ever built it would certainly be against the interests of these enterprises.

While William Sharon and other powers of the bank sat at conference planning strategy, Sutro was making contracts with mine owners that he was sure would enable him to start digging. His proposition was simple. He would drain the pesky hot water from their mines and even haul out their ores to the string of mills he would build along the Carson River — all this for free. Then for only $1 per ton he would mill all ores assaying up to $35 per ton, over that $2. The bargain was accepted by many, reluctantly by some, and Sutro agreed to start work by August 1, 1867, spending not less than $400,000 each year to speed completion of the tunnel.

He delayed only long enough to secure additional equipment and mules but the delay was disastrous. Sharon and other big men in the Comstock went to the mine owners, pointing out what to do if they knew what was good for them. So when Sutro was ready to start work, he found there was no money available and there would not be any, that almost every contract was being ignored.

DURING TUNNEL DIGGING DAYS large numbers of mules were used at Sutro, housed in this barn. Drilling and blasting equipment was hauled into dark tunnel by docile animals, each carrying own "headlight". Small building at entrance to tunnel was stocked with collar torches and oil, crew of young boys placing lighted torch in mule's collar as it entered, removing beacon as it emerged. Animals were invaluable to project, were well cared for, had good pasture along Carson River.

SUTRO AS IT APPEARS TODAY from site of mansion. In foreground are fireplace bricks and fancy metal cap which topped chimney. Blacksmith shop and warehouse show at right center. Tunnel opens at point about 200 feet this side of small buildings at extreme right. In distance is Carson Valley, river marked by trees.

Rather than sue, Sutro went to Washington where he appealed in vain to Congress for a subsidy. Sharon had already telegraphed representatives of the Bank of California in the capitol to block any move Sutro might make. Sutro tried to interest financiers William Astor and Commodore Vanderbilt and others only to be snubbed. Back in Nevada he tried to persuade legislators to put up money to start work already ratified by them but again the Sharon shadow stood in his way. As if the Bank of California were not enough to block his efforts, Sutro found another obstacle forming. A group called the "Big Four", Mackey, Fair, Flood

and O'Brien, bonanza kings of the Comstock, was becoming ever more powerful. These men also threw their weight against Sutro, recognizing in the projected tunnel a menace to their whole empire.

Then on April 7, 1869, tragedy struck in the Yellowjacket mine — fire that took the lives of forty-five men. Some members of the crew were rescued by raising them in the open "cage" but others died in the same operation, being so weak they fell against the sides of the shaft and were crushed by the rising platform. The rest, except for three who were actually burned to death, died of suffocation below. The disaster caused great feeling in Virginia City and Sutro took advantage of it, believing firmly that the proposed tunnel would avert future disasters like this by providing a means of escape.

On September 20 he made an impassioned speech for his project at Piper's Opera House. The reaction to the miners was overwhelmingly in favor of the tunnel, some even volunteering to lynch Sharon and the "Big Four". The ENTERPRISE, heretofore reluctant to print anything favoring the tunnel, now broke the speech across the entire front page. Popular sentiment was on Sutro's side and his project now had some backing. The miners even pledged enough funds so construction of the tunnel could begin October 19, 1869.

But even thousands of dollars supplied by miners were only a drop in the bucket compared to the millions needed, and the big money still had its feet planted solidly in the way. Congress eventually sent a commission to investigate the mines and the claimed need to run a tunnel to them. Of course the bank and the four Irishmen saw to it the committee of stuffed shirts never saw the steaming depths, never breathed air made intolerably fetid by heat, humidity, explosive fumes and sweating men. The investigators returned to Washington with the report that there was no real need for a tunnel, especially since the Virginia City powers had finished their railroad. Blow that this was, Sutro held stubbornly to the remaining benefits that would accrue.

Then came the first real money, $2,500,000, from McClamont's Bank in London, where Sutro had applied. Now began the pattern of going broke, getting money again, a succession lasting to completion of the tunnel 13 long years and $5 million later.

Even after the bore itself, twelve feet wide and nine feet high, had broken through to the bottom of the first mine, connecting branches to other mines must be built and a three-foot square trough laid down the middle to carry off the hot water

TOWN OF SUTRO about 1880. At extreme left is Sutro's mansion, rectangle of water beside it called by him an "artificial lake", by scoffers "Sutro's Frog Pond". It was aptly named, Sutro having stocked it first with fish and ducks, then insisted on bullfrogs also. These proving unavailable, not being native to western states, he settled for largest he could get. True bullfrogs have since populated Carson River, having been introduced much later. Warehouse building at right (with four windows on end) still stands as do many others. Courtesy Nevada State Museum.

TUNNEL OPENING 94 years after start of construction. Scene marks head of Tunnel Avenue, 200-foot wide thorough-fare down which passed ore cars headed for mill at foot. Also coming out of opening was steaming stream of water drained from deep mines of Comstock Lode. Water still gushes forth but from spring 2,000 feet back.

as promised. The trough would handle in one year alone, 1880, more than two billion gallons of steaming water.

Completion of the big job dealt a severe blow to the town of Sutro which was started to house and feed workmen. With construction crews laid off away went the town's main support. There was only the mill for processing tunnel-brought ores and the barns for housing mules used to draw ore carts through the bore. And Sutro continued for a time to live in the mansion he had built just above the tunnel.

But the sad fact was, by the time the long delayed Sutro tunnel was completed, the Comstock day of glory was ending. Royalties on ore hauled through it did pay the cost of building but that was about all. Sutro himself soon got out from under, the incentive of struggle gone. He sold his stock in the company and went on to other conquests in the city that was to be his home for the rest of his life — San Francisco.

The only residents of Sutro now are Robin Larson and his family. He writes: "I first saw the Sutro Tunnel site in the spring of 1959 on an automobile trip east with my father. At that time there was a caretaker. In the spring of 1962 I traveled to Nevada to see the Sutro Tunnel again and found it deserted with signs to the effect that it was destined to become a state park. The place interested

MULE PULLS LITTLE TRAIN carrying work crew from tunnel mouth about 1890. During construction days several attempts were made to use other power than mules. Horses failed, proving flighty and not tolerating heat. Mules worked longer in high temperatures until suddenly dropping dead as if shot. Most mechanical contrivances failed because of lack of ventilation causing fatal fumes to accumulate. Courtesy Nevada Historical Society.

me very much and it disturbed me to see that it was deserted. People were breaking and stealing things at such a rapid rate that there was a great change since I had seen it last. I decided to make a personal effort to protect it until it should become a park.

"With the cooperation of the Nevada State Park System and the Comstock Tunnel and Drainage Company (the owners) I took up residence at the tunnel portal and lived there for a year, protecting the place, cleaning it up and campaigning to make it into a state park. The state refused to accept Sutro and rather than see it destroyed and looted and because I had fallen in love with the place, the history and the country, I took up a lease and I intend to preserve the tunnel portal and the existing eighteen buildings as an historical monument. I don't want to restore, only to prevent any further decay."

SUTRO'S LARGE STAMP MILL stands at edge of Carson River valley. River is marked by willows, cottonwoods in middle distance. Ore cars entered building on level at right, tipped to disgorge contents toward left into maws of crushers. Mill is one of largest and best preserved in state. Interior, large and shadowy, still holds most of equipment. Visitors can peer inside, are advised against climbing stairs as treads are frail, floor boards shaky and unsafe.

IONE, NEVADA

"An Ione father who had passed incalculable sleepless nights has immortalized himself by discovering a method of keeping babies quiet. The modus operandi is as follows: set it up, propped by a pillow if it can not set alone and smear its fingers liberally with thick molasses. Then put a dozen feathers into its hands. It will then continue to pick the feathers from one hand to another until it falls asleep. As soon as it awakens again, more molasses and more feathers. In place of the nerve wracking yells there will be silence and enjoyment unspeakable."

Such heart-warming hints as this in the weekly NYE COUNTY NEWS were rarely needed to fill space for things were never very dull in Ione. In the early, flamboyant hectic days one rich discoverer followed another after the first one in April, 1863, by a disappointed Comstocker, P. A. Haven. His strike was made near the center of the Shoshone Range, a string of mountains running north and south as do most of Nevada's ranges. When the camp began to need a name, one erudite miner thought of Ione, the heroine in Bulwer Lytton's novel, "The Last Days of Pompeii".

In only a few short months enough hopeful prospectors had trekked up the Reese River from Austin to make a real town with all the trappings—saloons, stores, and many cabins, all thrown together with adobe, stone, brush or anything handy.

This motley collection grew and the citizens began clamoring to the legislature to have their town made the county seat. The authorities were willing but first had to create a new county for Ione to sit in. This was done by major surgery on two existing ones, Lander, and Esmeralda, carving hefty chunks from each to make the new Nye county. The august and liberal body of lawmakers even made available $800 for a courthouse.

The NYE COUNTY NEWS, published weekly in Ione during the summer of the following year, was a worker for progress in the mountain community. It ran a plug for a new stage line to Austin along Reese River: "The line is well stocked and has accommodating drivers and carries passengers and packages at a reasonable rate. It is not yet definitely settled as to what day it will run. We hope to carry an advertisement next week when we will tell all we know." The line came through with the ad next week. "STAGE FOR AUSTIN. The stage for Austin will leave at an early hour tomorrow, Sunday morning. Passengers, in order to secure a seat should book their names today." The next week, another item. "The stage has established its office at the Bellrude store. It will leave at its usual early hour tomorrow."

Then the lively weekly turned its efforts to securing a bank and assay office for Ione. "A GOOD OPENING" was the headline, and the editorial:

PRIMITIVE CONSTRUCTION dates from 1860s in many Ione buildings. These walls are two feet thick, cracks between roughly cut stones chinked with mud. Roof was covered with clay, mud and layer of gravel.

RAFTERS OF PRECIOUS SAWN LUMBER support heavy horizontal layer of lighter brush which is in turn covered with a thick layer of mud and gravel. Interior was once neatly lined with muslin, vestiges of which interfered with picture taking. Photographer moved aside ancient cloth and got heavy shower of dust on camera and face. Available light came from tiny, deep-set windows and small open door.

"Now that our town is making such rapid strides toward prosperity, we would suggest to some enterprising individual the start of a small banking house in connection with an assay office. There appears to be plenty of money in this community but a scarcity of change, and as work progresses in the various mines rich discoveries are made, which for lack of a competent assay office, their capacity is unknown." And the happy note was sounded two weeks later:

"LONG AWAITED ASSAY OFFICE OPENS by Thomas Cahill, five years assayer in San Francisco mint. We welcome him in our town, having waited a long time for something of this kind. Bring in your specimens!"

There was always room for one more saloon and the newspaper held out the glad hand. "NEW SALOON. W. A. Brophy, Esquire, one of the old settlers returned to our place yesterday with a large stock of liquor. He proposes opening a saloon in the old stand formerly occupied by the Fashion Saloon, next door to the News office. We shall be around, Billy, and 'sample'." And the next week's spread: "INTERNATIONAL SALOON OPENS — BIG FANFARE — FREE DRINKS."

The editor, having accepted payment for this ad

in trade, was incapacitated for several days but rose valiantly to announce: "To Mrs. Michael Kelly we are under obligations for a plate of nice, fresh butter. We carried it to our cabin and our better ? half pronounced it A No. 1. Mrs. Kelly keeps a large dairy and furnishes our citizens with fresh milk and butter. We are glad to learn that she has a large custom."

And then the enterprising editor got apple hungry. "Grocer Bellrude says he has a large stock of fresh apples but as we have not seen any around the office, we have to take his word for it." Apparently Mr. Bellrude was properly rebuked for, a few weeks later came the enlightening information: "Happening into Bellrude's store yesterday we observed a large amount of flour, sugar and such like stowed away as if he was laying in a good winter's supply."

Theatrical news was not neglected. "The beautiful comedy, 'The Swiss Cottage', and a laughable farce, 'The Cobbler and the Lord', will be presented at the Ione Theater. Open 7½ o'clock, start 8, adm. 50c." And always among these lively notes was mining news. "On Saturday last the men engaged in sinking a shaft upon the Olive Ledge discovered a large deposit of gold-bearing quartz which

SOME EARLY CABINS were built of logs formed from nut pine trees and junipers dragged down from higher elevations. Trees are of small size and gnarly growth, logs short and knotty. Chimney is of roughly fired brick, possibly done in hot bonfire. By 1865 commercial kiln was established at nearby Union. Some claim this structure was first courthouse.

will realize $8,000 to $9,000 a ton. The outfit is called the Knickerbocker Mining Co."

The hard working editor evidently took time out occasionally to view the passing parade and voice his observations: "There are many strange faces on the street and it is not unusual to have them pointed out as capitalists" . . . "Emigrant trains still through our town, bound for California. A large train from Davis Cy, Iowa, passed through last night. They are headed for Sonoma Cy. California. They report a very pleasant trip, although there were some delays due to Indian attacks." . . . "Everyone in the city is hard at work. There are no idle men and the streets seem almost deserted in the daytime." . . .

"IONE LIVELY — from the number of teams seen on our streets during the week several times we have blinked our eyes and imagined ourselves on C Street in Virginia before the San Francisco bears got control of the mines." . . . "EVERYBODY COMING, to look at the mines. So many make plans to remain permanently Ione sees a brilliant future ahead."

But it was not to be. Ione's gold proved to be shallow, was soon exhausted and the town with the classic name was just another flash in the pan, as were so many other Nevada mining camps. It had been in the spring of 1863 that the first discovery was made, the spring of 1864 when Ione was made the county seat and the spring of 1867 when that honor was taken away and bestowed on an upstart fifty miles away — Belmont. What really hurt was Belmont's being populated largely with Ione people, miners and prospectors who had defected to the new strike on the old theory that gold is always shinier in the other fellow's claim.

Ione was slow to accept the inevitable. The newspaper of April 6, 1867, reported the county official would complete removal of county records to the new seat at Belmont "as soon as the citizens have reconciled themselves to the fact that they have lost the county seat fight."

Although staggered by the blow, and much shriveled in population, Ione managed to keep from dying entirely, even to the present day. Some small or large discovery has at intervals revivified it

PRICKLY "DESERT POPPY" blooms profusely in Ione streets, is properly called Argemone. Various parts of showy annual plant have emetic, narcotic properties. White petals have crinkled, satiny look, are centered by cluster of yellow stamens, flower being about six inches across.

MANY OLD BUGGIES AND WAGONS indicate remoteness of Ione. In old camps of more convenient access, such relics have been taken by vandals, wheels removed and carried off. Backlighting here brings out details of sagebrush and wheels.

enough to hold a few people there. Up to 1880 the mines turned out a million dollars in gold and silver, a small figure compared to the production in the few big years.

One development kept things going for a few years. In 1907 a ledge of cinnabar was discovered in the hills just east of town. Its bright red color should have attracted attention years before but in those days gold was all anyone could see. Silver was recognized grudgingly later, it being so much harder to extract than free gold.

Immediately, upon finding the cinnabar, horizontal roasting furnaces were constructed to melt the mercury or "quicksilver" out of the ore. Fuel was mostly fast burning but plentiful sage brush. More substantial pine was brought down from high elevations after most of the brush had been cleared from slopes nearby. In the several years of operation, some 11,000 flasks of mercury were produced.

Today the town is very quiet, only a few residents hanging on, barely enough to keep up Ione's resolve to "never say die" — and they do miss the old editor.

GRANTSVILLE, NEVADA

On a cold and snowy day in February 1881, a frightened Mexican miner sat in a tunnel shivering. The tunnel was one dug into the mountains at the mining camp of Grantsville which had proved barren of gold and made useful as a jail. It was cold in the tunnel but the Mexican was trembling for another reason. He was charged with the murder of a fellow worker the night before and he was afraid Grantsville citizens, fired up with Shoshone Mountain hooch, would not wait for legal justice.

He was right. The heavy tunnel door crashed in and the roaring mob of miners made for him, the lead man carrying a rope. Pedro was hustled off to the stamp mill, hoisted up on a massive timber, the rope thrown over a higher one, noose slipped over his head. One push and the luckless man was swinging in the wind.

A coroner's jury next day named several persons thought guilty of the lynching. When questioned by the sheriff, the spokesman gave their reason for the

DWELLING IS BUILT of native, uncut stone. Some pains were taken to place flattened side outward for neater effect. Roof was of usual brush construction over poles, thick layer of mud plastered overall. "Airtight" tin heater in center of single room provided heat and cooking surface. Fuel was brush and pine wood.

LITTLE RED BRICK SCHOOLHOUSE supposedly had capacity of sixty pupils, but for this number interior seems cramped. Elegantly proportioned fireplace occupies left end. When supply of pupils dwindled, building was converted into boarding house, with kitchen at left, sleeping space gained by addition of shed at right.

action. The previous August another murderer had been arrested and tried in a legal manner. He was judged guilty but instead of the death sentence he was sent to the state prison where he was serving out an ordinary life sentence. The Mexican had been lynched to avoid his receiving similar soft treatment. The explanation was accepted and the incident forgotten.

The discoverer of gold in Grantsville was P. A. Haven, the same prospector who had located the first vein in Ione. Here he immediately organized a mining district and laid out a town. When eager miners came in droves, Haven was ready for them, selling them lots from $50 to $500. Whatever made the difference in the price, it was not the view, for all the lots had that if nothing else. "Grantsville is laid out," read an early description, "in a beautiful canyon" — a gross understatement. The steep canyon walls were covered with a heavy growth of nut pine trees, the predominant forest cover of the area and altitude. Later all the trees were cut down for fuel, shoring and charcoal.

Haven seemed to be more interested in discovering potential wealth and promoting it than in making any development. His original claim was worked out soon after he left and the place languished almost to a ghost town before it was ever well established. In September 1877, a representative of the Alexander Company, a big mining firm, traveled the seventy dusty miles from Austin and had a look around. He acquired the property for the company, set to work to develop it and Grantsville soon began to look like the town it had started out to be.

There were two general merchandise stores, hardware and tin shop, a livery stable, blacksmith shop, two barber shops and a jewelry store. The town also boasted of two assay offices, a bank, furniture store, two drug stores and a fine restaurant. As usual, saloons outnumbered all others — twelve. Not mentioned in the factual report were bawdy houses but the camp would not have been unique in this respect.

Three weekly newspapers spoke for the area, a succession starting with the NYE COUNTY NEWS in

1867. It made out for about two years, was supplanted by the GRANTSVILLE SUN which lasted only one year when replaced by the GRANTSVILLE BONANZA.

The gold and silver in the Grantsville mining district were found in veins of porphyry, limestone and quartz running northwest to southeast, dipping into the earth at an angle. Other metals were there in variety, such as lead, antimony and copper. Milling was done by crushing and roasting according to information dated 1881, but other methods came in later as is evidenced by old flotation and paddle vats still in the ruins of one mill.

There was plenty of wood, a heavy stand of nut pine trees being ravished for fuel, and plenty of water the year around from several good springs.

All food and supplies were freighted in from Austin at a cost of $40 a ton. Most perishable foods were not obtainable in hot weather because of spoilage or in winter when roads were impassable. Some butter and milk were obtained from Ione where there was a dairy. Occasionally someone would attempt to keep chickens but imported grain was too expensive to make this practical. Also hen houses had to have some heat in winter, otherwise eggs froze in the nest, as did chickens' feet on the roosts at night.

Although Grantsville held tighter to prosperity than did her sister Ione, her death was complete when it came. The town has been deserted for many years, is today one of Nevada's loneliest ghost towns.

EXTENSIVE RUINS of mining operations remain in Grantsville. In extreme foreground is up-ended two-holer. Behind is mess hall for miners and mill workers, with kitchen attached at left. At right of, and behind mess hall, are ruins of stamp mill. Extending upwards are various sections of mill. Recovery here was done at least in part by floatation, vats still in lower section. Principal mines were Alexander which had shaft 1200 feet deep and Brooklyn. Young pines make gallant attempt to reforest denuded hills but progress is slow in short growing season.

BERLIN & UNION, NEVADA

The past of this ghost town goes back some 100 million years, not to gold but to the amphibious animals, *Ichthyosaurs*. Berlin had gold but along with it the fossil remains of these "fish lizards" or more accurately water creatures akin to whales. Harold and Dorothy Newman will explain them successfully. They are the only residents of Berlin and are responsible for the preservation of the relics.

Berlin is easy to find. Unlike many ghost towns, hidden away in some brush-grown gulch, adobe or rock walls melting into the mother earth from which they sprang, Berlin's bones are gaunt frame structures, worn and weathered but defiantly erect and stand out boldly in a substantial group conspicuous

for miles. Further dramatizing the old camp is the backdrop of Mt. Berlin rising to a height of 9,081 feet above sea level. Set high on the flank of the Shoshone Range and seen from a distance of several miles across a flat, dusty basin the dead town seems still pulsing with robust blood of yesterday. But it isn't. The buildings are only hollow shells without doors, the windows staring without glass. Only these and the Newmans.

The agatized remains of the marine creatures were interesting to the more knowledgeable prospectors from 1860 on. Possibly the first printed mention of the fossil finds appeared in the July 29, 1865 issue of the NYE COUNTY NEWS, published in

PARTS OF SKELETON of huge ichthyosaur, turned to agate-like substance after millions of years of burial, are exposed but left in place by student paleontologists directed by Dr. Charles L. Camp of University of California during four year period following spring of 1953. In foreground are pelvic bones; extreme left is fetus; left center, vertebrae. Tail of twenty-five foot amphibian stretches into background. Altogether nineteen large ichthyosaurs have been uncovered in limey shale. Guardian of deposits, Harold Newman, when asked about future excavations said they are uncertain because of short political tenure of interested officials. "By the time they learn to pronounce 'ichthyosaur' they're out of office."

BUNK HOUSE for Berlin mine workers seems to have been dropped on the ground. In many early mining camps violence often erupted in bunkhouses where drinking and gambling was carried on in evenings, but Berlin seems to have no records of murder or lynching at camp.

Ione, a short distance from Berlin. "Several of the boys have been bringing in to this editor some strange specimens for this country so far from the ocean. They are enough to make one think that perhaps this whole area was once covered with water, even to the mountain tops where the shells were found. They are indeed objects of study for the curious."

It was not until 1928 that the stony bones received official recognition, when a faculty member of Leland Stanford University made public their importance. Later Geologist Margaret Wheat exposed more fossils with simple hand tools. She interested Dr. Charles L. Camp, distinguished paleontologist in the possibilities of an on-site exhibit. The Museum of Paleontology, University of California, carried on delicate but extensive excavation work from 1953 to 1957 and Dr. Camp was successful in

getting the State of Nevada to designate the area a state park.

The name ichthyosaur translates "fish lizard" but the animal was neither. One miner-historian describes the geneology as a "cross between a shark and a whale", a biological impossibility. Actually the animals were entirely warm blooded with some of the characteristics of the modern whales and porpoises, and except for whales and some forms of prehistoric dinosaurs, were the largest form of life known, reaching a length of sixty feet. They swam in warm waters which once filled the great basin, having their existence in the beginning of the "age of reptiles", the Middle Triassic, some 200 million years ago.

The particular group whose petrified remains came to light near Berlin seems to have suffered the same fate of whales today. They were beached and since the animals had a lightly constructed rib cage

SHELL OF COOK HOUSE stands next to mine dumps at Berlin. Large wood burning stove was carried out years ago, possibly to permit other use for building. While photo was being taken Newman's retriever entertained by flushing and chasing dozens of large jackrabbits which bounded back and forth in front of camera as though feeling spirit of game.

and not able to protect the lungs out of water, their enormous weight caused collapse and death. They sank into deep primordial ooze, flesh decaying and bones becoming fossilized. About 60 million years ago the whole area was covered by volcanic flows, then much later the protective stratum split and erosion began, exposing some of the bones.

The deposits lie on a bench directly above a canyon holding other remains—those of the once thriving mining camp of Union, about two miles south and east of Berlin. Union owed its origin to P. A. Haven's discoveries as did Ione, Grantsville and Berlin in 1863. In common also with its sister towns, Union had an initial boom of all too brief a duration, then several spurts of energy equally short.

An item from the NYE COUNTY NEWS of Ione, July 8, 1865, said: "The first lot of bullion from the Union district amounting to about 200 pounds was shipped from the Pioneer Mills. We hope next week to give a larger figure." Next week's issue failed to carry any figure at all but there was a pat on the back for Union, a generous gesture considering the traditional rivalry between the two camps. "There is much doing at Union. It promises to rival our town. We congratulate the Union boys upon their prosperity."

About a year after Union's beginning, a Mr. Shobe, while prospecting the area, came across a large deposit of clay. Shobe could see an indirect glitter of "gold" in the material, found where there

ADOBE BUILDING only substantial ruin at Union. Roof has preserved it from complete deterioration, will soon give way. Search up and down long canyon revealed many fragmentary signs of occupation by hundreds of miners and store keepers.

was no lumber which was always a fire hazard. He abandoned all further prospecting, took a claim on the site and set about getting capital to build a large kiln. His first big job was not for house building material, though, as the NEWS stated: "Mr. Shobe of Union has taken the contract to burn 100,000 bricks for the Atlantic and Pacific Construction Co. to be used in constructing a large roasting furnace for their mill." Several brick buildings using Shobe's product remain at Grantsville, including the school house and mess halls at the mill.

Just below the enclosure containing the ichthyo-saur exhibits is the camp set up by excavation crews composed mostly of men students interested in the work. It took advantage of several old buildings remaining from Union's lusty days and added a few ingenious improvements. Coming in from work, covered with dust and perspiration, the men used a unique bathing arrangement. Water from an icy cold spring was conveyed to a metal tank near quarters, the sun heating it during the day to usable temperature. Immediately below the tank a bath tub was placed and connected to the tank. It is included in the park camp grounds and campers are free to use it, if privacy is not required. This fact usually confines the use to small fry whose mothers are glad to remove a few layers of road dust from the young hides.

ROCKLAND, NEVADA

Joseph Wilson had an exciting life on the ranches and in the mines of Nevada. He died at ninety-four, leaving voluminous notes and memoirs among them the story of the founding of Pine Grove and its newer, smaller neighbor, Rockland. "On September first of 1863," he wrote, "my father, David Wilson, and uncle William Wilson, bought the squatter's rights to the Wheeler farm, consisting of 4,000 acres, for $2,000."

This was unsurveyed land on which Pat Wheeler and his seven sons had squatted under Utah law in 1860, on the west fork of the Walker river in the extreme south end of Mason valley. The Wheelers had erected earth boundary mounds, three years being allowed to fence the land. Once on it, young William Wilson was eager to go prospecting in the Pine Grove mountains, included in the ranch, but his older brother and family persuaded him to stay, help get part of the land under cultivation and start a herd of cattle. David, however, was just as anxious to find out about mineral wealth and allowed his young brother to saddle a horse once in a while and have a look around.

Of the Paiute Indians who came to the ranch begging food, most persistent was a family trio—Hog-or-Die Jim who sometimes chopped wood, his wife Hog-or-Die Mary who did the washing and their son "Bummer Charlie" who "never did anything useful". To this family, Hog-or-Die meant something like "eat high on the hog or starve."

MILL WAS ONCE much more extensive. Fire, bruising weight of snows, vandals and time have all taken toll. Stone walls date from earliest period, cement foundations coming later.

**CONE OF NUT PINE Pinus Mono-
phylla,** showing several "nuts" still
attached. Cones are formed during
summer, remain as small prickly
balls until following season when
growth is rapid. Late in second
summer green cone is solid, hard
and dripping with sparkling, clear,
fragrant pitch or resin. In September they begin to open and shed
seeds. Nuts were once staple article of diet for Indians who beat
limbs with sticks to bring cones
down. Fire was built over heaps of
cones which caused quick opening
of scales and release of nuts. Heat
also dissipated small quantity of
turpentine which made unroasted
nuts bitter and inedible.

When they came to the ranch one day, David had no wood to be chopped so brought out a chunk of gold ore showing definite flecks of the yellow metal. He asked Hog-or-Die Jim in a jumble of Paiute and sign language: "Do you know where there is any more rock like this?" The Indian indicated he did and pointed out a location in the hills above the ranch, three and a half miles south of Mt. Etna in the Pine Grove mountains.

David now turned William loose with abandon and after some diligent search he found a gold deposit. The Wilsons then gave their full attention to mining. From the time the find was made in 1866 to about 1871 Pine Grove developed to a population of over 1,000. The three original arrastras owned by Portuguese Joe grew to several power stamp mills using steam from boilers fired by nut pine wood. The ore was known as "free-milling", the easiest type of work, needed only to be washed and crushed in sluices. In later years a mill was built to rework some of the waste, but most of the gold had been recovered by the cruder method.

The town was a boisterous one. (Ed: this infor-mation differs sharply from that gathered earlier which declared the Wilsons to be "Blue Nose", meaning intolerant of drinking or gambling, that miners went to nearby Rockland for diversion). See Pine Grove, WESTERN GHOST TOWNS. Joseph Wilson relates that Pine Grove had two sections, that "there were five saloons in the upper part and three in the lower, with a dance hall in the middle". There were also three hotels, Wells Fargo office and a large general store. The barber shop and shoeshine parlor was operated by a colored man who charged fifty cents for a haircut, twenty-five for a shine. The post office charged three cents for sending a letter in competition with the express company which charg-ed an exhorbitant five.

With so many people drawn to an area where a few years before there had been no one, the surrounding hills got a close examination for precious metals. And in 1869 a Pine Grove resident, a Mr. Keene, found a rich vein of silver and gold three and a half miles from his home. As quickly as he could he built a quartz mill in Bridgeport Can-yon just below his mine. He called the lively little town that grew up around the mine and mill Rock-land, presumably for the fantastic and beautiful red rock cliffs towering over the location.

Keene had trouble keeping his expenses below his money intake. His men were paid irregularly

LITTLE ROCKLAND LODGING HOUSE, once painted bright red, is faded but still upright. In back is large sleeping porch, open to breezes which at this altitude are considerable and the snows which are deep and long lasting. Nut pines show needle arrangement and bark texture.

and when no money was forthcoming they set up a howl. One in particular, a Mr. Rhodes, trouble maker at best, threatened to get even and when Keene was away raising money for the payroll, Rhodes set fire to the mill. He was arrested, convicted of arson and sent to the state prison. Keene got deeper in debt, finally lost control of the mine and ex-Gov. Blaisedell tried his hand at operating it and also failed. Then C. D. Lane stepped in, got some ore out but he too was unsuccessful. The mine was deserted and Tom Flynn stayed on as watchman for years, at length buying an interest in the claim and running some ore through the mill.

During this period a boulder showing chunks of gold and weighing several hundred pounds was found nearby. It assayed $500 to the ton and created great excitement. The chunk was definitely a huge piece of float from some rich lode near the area. Hordes of prospectors tried to locate the source but all failed and Rockland settled back to doze again.

The Lyon County Times of Nov. 24, 1894, re-

ported this item: FATAL ACCIDENT AT PINE GROVE. Last Monday morning between 8 and 9, John Redding, who was working on the Wilson tailing dump in Pine Grove, was caved upon and buried under tons of dirt. As soon as the accident happened, a force of men began to dig for the unfortunate man. After several tons of dirt had been removed, the body was found but life had been crushed out of it. The deceased was a native of Missouri, aged 26 and came to Nevada about 5 years ago. He leaves a father, three sisters and two brothers. The funeral took place Thursday at the Grove and was largely attended."

By 1948 Tom Flynn was thoroughly discouraged over his property, cleaned his little cabin and headed his old car down the mountain grade to think things over in town — maybe raise money or abandon the pesky thing. Just as Flynn drove into the canyon where the road in the defile is extremely steep, rocky and narrow, a torrent of rain he later termed as a "water spout" struck the rocky walls. The deluge of muddy water took out all semblance of road and carried Flynn and the car down into the gulch. He spent fourteen hours, he said, in reaching the town. No mind searching was needed.

The decision had been reached. Tom Flynn kept driving on to leave his now inaccessible perch in the Pine Grove mountains to the buzzards.

MINER'S CABIN is typical of most homes remaining in Rockland and other mountain mining camps. This one seemed to belong to bottle collector. Photo was made in August and shows nut pine cones in windrows, having fallen during gales of previous winter. All nuts have been harvested by squirrels, birds, mice and other rodents.

AURORA, NEVADA

Angus McLeod crossed the plains in 1856-57. The journey lasted six months and included his helping to drive 1200 head of cattle from Dover, Arkansas, working in the California placer mines, farming, clerking in a Genoa, Nevada, store. After this devious circuit he settled on land near Yerington, Nevada, in 1862.

The land extended a mile and a half along the Walker River and he was hardly established before trouble began. Three men — Lee, Mills and Greely — built a flour mill just below the McLeod land, constructing a stout dam and digging a ditch to convey water to power the mill wheel.

As water rose behind the new dam it flooded the land above to a depth of several feet, Angus McLeod's ranch included. Determined to avoid it being turned into a lake, he cut an outlet for the river water to flow around the dam and drain his land. This resulted in the mill ditch running dry and filling with sand.

Lee, Mills and Greely were blazing mad, bringing suit and a year-long legal hassle. The first skirmish ended in success for the mill men but at the conclusion of the trial, McLeod was the victor. Both sides however were drained of cash. Angus leased the ranch to Charles Martin and with his wife went up to the roaring camp of Aurora. He owned an interest in the big Wingate Hotel which had stores and lodge hall on the ground level, and he also owned a lumber yard and the toll road extending from Wellington.

Aurora had sprung up almost overnight. In August, 1860, a prospecting party composed of J. M. Corey, James N. Braley and E. R. Hicks stopped to let their horses forage in a grassy little gulch well watered by Antelope Creek which came out of nut pine covered hills. All three men took their picks to the surrounding rock outthrusts. Braley and Corey had come over the Sierra from San Jose, California, had looked over the ground at Virginia City where they met Hicks. They were too late at the Comstock but not on Antelope Creek. Hicks, a part Cherokee, chipped off the first piece of glittering rock near the top of the hill. Corey found his treasure about the same time and in a day or so the three had located four claims. Next morning when the rising sun colored the entire eastern sky in a blaze of glory, the imaginative Corey tossed out the name of the location — "Aurora, Goddess of the Dawn."

The three founders of the lofty camp did not stay long. Corey and Braley made 357 mining claims, selling them in two months for $30,000, then departed for California to plant fruit trees near Santa Clara. On his departure for home in Arkansas, Hicks carried $10,000 in his poke.

When the three waved goodby to the town they did not leave it deserted. It was already populated with a motley crowd that had rushed in at the first news of the strikes. Almost before these men could start working their claims they had to have shelter and threw together whatever was at hand fast, for at that altitude of 7,741 feet, winter came early and snow sifted down among the pines. Houses were first mostly dugouts with stone fronts, roofed with brush and mud. The first business establishment, owned by one Pat Hickey, was fabricated of "sticks, stones, shakes, canvas and mud." Crude as they

OLD ETCHING OF EXCHANGE HOTEL from "History of Nevada" by Thompson and West. This is same building which Angus McLeod bought about 1880 and was later burned by revengeful arsonists. Front, facing Antelope Street, was fancy, 1910 photo showing plain side and rear.

RARE PICTURE OF AURORA made by "Scotty" McLeod about 1910 while on prospecting trip. Town has nostalgic memories for him, being born in Dunlap house at far end of Antelope Street which angles across lower left in photo. House has dormer, is trimmed white. Road leads right to workings of Esmeralda Lode, discovered on afternoon of Aug. 25, 1860, by J. M. Corey. Below mine is small group of mine buildings, one of which is only brick structure remaining. In central foreground on Antelope Street is burned out shell of Exchange Hotel, that street continuing on down through old Chinese quarter to become road to Bodie, Calif. Route is no longer passable, only entry at left through Fletcher, which road passes Aurora cemetery at top of hill.

were, stores and saloons were well patronized by thirsty miners. A few slugs of Aurora Lightning and nobody worried what the walls were made of as long as they stayed still.

Every bit of food, every pound of explosives, in fact every item necessary to work or life itself, had to come in over rough trails on the backs of mules. Even after a semblance of a road came in from Bodie, wagons were sure to break a wheel on a rock or get mired in deep mud. Prices for everything were sky high and the estimated keep for a mule $3 a day.

The Angus McLeod family first lived at the Dunlap House at the upper end of Antelope Street and later on, April 29, 1878 their son Charles was born there. Now, at 86, Charles or "Scotty" as he is affectionately known all over Nevada, lives in Yerington. He is alert, witty and after a lifetime of mining activity is a mine of information and anecdotes about the state's boisterous early days.

"We lived in the Dunlap House only a short time," Scotty relates, "and then father bought the Exchange Hotel farther down the street where we lived in upper floor rooms. I was little more than a baby then. One of the roomers had three canary birds, a novelty in that rough town, and went on a short vacation, leaving the birds in mother's care. She went in to feed them once and found me there. Two of the little things were already dead on the floor and I had the third in my fist, squeezing the life out of it. When mother asked me what in the world I was doing, I told her: "I'm making them sing, mama." Scotty proves this with the old hotel ledger. Item in column of expense, dated Dec. 21, 1881 — "Three birds, $30."

Meanwhile the three losers in the lawsuit against Angus McLeod were still smarting with resentment. Charles noticed one day that his friend the Chinese cook for the hotel was missing, a strange white man in his place. That night the family was awakened with the Exchange Hotel in flames. All occupants escaped in time, most of the men in their underwear, leaving six-shooters and ammunition behind. As all stood outside watching flames engulf the hotel, bullets in guns and cartridge boxes began to explode, the air full of flying lead.

Investigation later showed that the Lee brothers and Greely had arranged the substitution of cooks, the new man pouring "coal oil" over the floors and igniting it. The hotel was completely gutted and never entirely rebuilt. The McLeod family moved again, this time to the toll house at the end of the road where Charles' brother Neil was born. The road in those days came in from the notorious Bodie, California, passing through Del Monte on the way and where it entered Aurora at the lower end of Antelope Street was a Chinese section. Asked if it contained the usual joss and gambling houses, Scotty replied: "Oh, no. They were all very fine people, industrious vegetable growers. Of course they may have had those things in another section of town but if so, I was too young to know about them."

Prowling about a shed at the toll house one day, young Charles found a box of dynamite percussion caps on a shelf. He dislodged them with a stick and the box fell to the floor, scattering the caps in all directions.

In playing with them he heard the call to lunch and popped one into his mouth as he ran. When he climbed up in the high chair he spit the cap out on the floor. The hired girl, Josie Hernleben, picked it up took a pin out of her blouse and poked at the white percussion dot in the bottom of the lethal cap. "There was a terrific explosion," Scotty said. "Josie's thumb and forefinger were blown off and stuck to the ceiling. No one ate much lunch that day."

When Charles was a little over eight years old the family moved down to the ranch, remaining there many years. As the boy grew up he followed the prospector's trail as did many other young fellows of the day. One of his buddies was J. C. Bray, with whom he later made the first claims in what was to be the fabulous camp of Rawhide.

Aurora was destined to suffer a long time from a unique problem. It wasn't sure just where it was. No one knew if the town lay completely in California, or in the Territory of Utah or whether it straddled the line. During the first winter a petition was presented to the California legislature, asking for the creation of a new county just for Aurora, so as to "release us from the hated laws and restrictions of Utah." By spring the California authorities concluded that since nobody knew just where the line was, they would arbitrarily include the new county, which held out such juicy prospects for taxes, in the state. Mono County was created in March, 1861, with Aurora as the county seat, a full set of county officials installed.

By April as weather improved, the real rush for the new camp set in and by June the residential total was 1,400 and increasing each day. When not a year old, town lots were selling for as much as $1,500. Four brickyards were started in the canyon and one of the first brick buildings was a schoolhouse, there being eighty children. That summer the first stamp mill was built, replacing several Mexican arrastras. By 1864 there were eighteen mills.

The summer of 1862 saw several outbreaks of Civil War antagonism. Southern sympathizers gathered in "underground" meeting places while Union organizations were more open, forming two groups— Esmeralda Rangers and Hooker Rifles. The fledgling city also had a newspaper, the ESMERALDA STAR and on August 23, 1862 it reported: "The Dixie group made a complete pandemonium of our town and continued their hideous orgies until late on Saturday morning, cheering Jeff Davis, Stonewall Jackson and the Southern Confederacy." The town was definitely on the Union side however. When the telegraph brought the astounding news of the assassination of President Lincoln, the whole town was "wrapped in gloom and tears rushed from the eyes of young men and old."

One dissenter, A. G. Judeigh, was so bold as to assert—"Lincoln was a tyrant and ought to have been dead long ago." Unfortunately for him the remark was carried to Captain Kelly who asked the Esmeralda Rangers to arrest Judeigh. He was placed in confinement with the immediate prospect of being taken to "Fort Churchill to carry sand." Under this threat he recanted, took the oath of allegiance and was discharged. He made a wise decision as he would have had to carry a fifty pound sack of sand on his back, marching up and down the parade ground in front of a soldier who would have corrected any loitering with the jab of a bayonet.

And all the time the ferment of Aurora's position went on. Far from settling the trouble, the California action only added fire to the dispute. A new group called Esmeralda Union Club spoke openly of being "California secessionists" and fought to get Aurora over the line into what was by this time Nevada, that Territory having been sliced off Utah. The solution of the wrangle caused a situation unlike any other known. Aurora, the seat of Mono

ONE OF MANY STAMP MILL RUINS persists at lower end of canyon, beside washed out road to Bodie. Aurora is in zone of transition between growth of sage brush and nut pines, specimens of both seen in background. Surrounding hills, several hundred feet higher, are heavily forested. Not many trees seen in 1910 photo, having been used for fuel for steam boilers providing power for many mills. Smaller trees have again covered hills.

County, California, now became the seat of Esmeralda County, Nevada, as well. Mining affairs were
delegated to Nevada courts, litigations connected
with franchises on roads and utilities were handled
under California jurisdiction. Private quarrels
could, at the discretion of those involved, be taken
either to Esmeralda's Judge Turner or Mono County's Judge Baldwin.

Soon after this dual arrangement was put into
effect, a general election was held and Aurora citizens had a choice. A resident could be registered in
California or Nevada or both. He could vote the
Republican ticket at one polling place (for California, the police station) and the Democratic at
the Nevada end of town (City Armory) or vice
versa, or vote the same ticket at both places. The
situation suggests a Roman holiday with twenty-
two stops along the way where a man could refresh
himself. It was remarked the town's bistros did their
biggest business that election day, a fact apparently
more important than being able to vote for a state
and territory at the same time.

The situation, amusing to some, intolerable to
others, was brought to an end by a survey party in
September, 1863, when Aurora was irrevocably
placed on the Nevada side with a good three miles
to spare. Bodie remained securely in California by
a five-mile margin. Finally convinced that their
position was now untenable, Mono officials in
Aurora packed their things and departed for Bridgeport, which replaced Aurora as the county seat.
With them went all money collected and left behind
were all outstanding warrants for some $20,000 in-
debtedness.

Aurora was still behaving like a mining camp.
During the halcyon days of heavy gold production,
bullion was shipped out on stages, duly recorded as
loaded. Even to this day skeptics maintain that the
return stage brought back the same gold to be re-
loaded and rerecorded. If this were so, it was done
by sharp design. High records of production from
certain mines boosted the value of stock. Express
company records list shipments in 1869, for example, as $27 million. This could have been accur-
ate but whatever the figure, there was a lot of bullion
on the move—certainly enough to rouse desire on the
part of highwaymen. Holdups were frequent and
occasionally a stage driver was killed.

There was even a "crime boss" in town, one
John Daley, secure in his position as the head of
a gang of thugs. Not knowing any better, W. R.
Johnson, a vegetable grower on the Walker River
shot and killed one of Daley's men, James Sears
for stealing a horse from him. It is not entirely clear
whether Johnson himself did the shooting or sent
one of his hands, John Rogers, to do it. But the
thief was dead and Johnson was responsible. Daley
was not the type to overlook the incident and vowed
to get Johnson.

His opportunity came soon, when Johnson came
into town with a load of vegetables. Daley gathered
his henchmen and waylaid the farmer in a dark
alley. First, Daley knocked Johnson down, then
shot him. Gangster William cut his throat and
"Three Fingered" Jack went through the victim's
pockets while James Masterson poured kerosene
over him and set his clothes on fire. By this time
Johnson's mistake was definitely paid for.

But the executioner had overdone it this time.
Aurora was already a little touchy about its record
of twenty-seven unpunished murderers and this last
atrocity was enough to trigger reaction. Some 350
citizens gathered in a hall in the Wingate Hotel
organized a vigilante committee which quickly
gathered in Daley and his crowd. All were thrown
into jail and guarded closely while a coroner's jury
deliberated. It was over like that. The four were
found guilty and sentenced to death on the gallows

All saloons were closed for the affair, mines were shut down and stamp mills ceased to chatter, the gallows was ready and execution only an hour away. Someone decided Governor Nye ought to know what was going on and so informed him by wire. The governor immediately responded that there must be no violence, that law and order must be preserved. Laconic was the telegraphed message to Governor Nye. "All quiet and orderly. Four men to be hung in half an hour." And they were. All the gallery had the help of brandy to sustain them, two being so well sustained they had to be held up. After that day, Aurora was somewhat more peaceful for a few months.

It was reported at one time that Aurora had 'seven hundred and sixty-one houses of which sixty-four are brick". In 1864 there were 6,000 people living in the town, the top population a few years later said to be 10,000. There was a fine brick courthouse, the ESMERALDA STAR was joined by another newspaper, the AURORA TIMES, many hotels, rooming houses and stores, almost all built of brick or stone. The first structures used bricks imported from as far as Sacramento, it was reported. Scotty McLeod says that after that a kiln was built and "bricks were baked right there in the canyon."

And Scotty settles another question, was the 'Mark Twain' cabin which was sent to Idlewild Park in Reno actually the one occupied by the famous humorist during his short stay in Aurora? He says: "The Dunlap House where I was born still stands at the upper end of Antelope Street. Directly across from it was the Mark Twain cabin. I often played in it as a child before it was removed to Idlewild Park." The defense rests.

When Aurora began to decline it went fast. Golden bonanzas had been genuine enough but shallow. Mines never went very deep, less than a hundred feet. The $30 million in gold and silver had been scraped off by the 70's. Though mining continued after that in desultory fashion, the glory that was Aurora's had faded. The tenure of the McLeod's just covered the waning period for when the family returned to the ranch almost everyone else left too.

Scotty furnishes another bit about the use of brick in Aurora. His friends Vic and James Bernard, whose family had lived in the town, recently visited there and found an opening to the old sewer lines. They were built entirely of brick, arched at the top which was high enough to allow a man to stand up. Unused for years, the lines ran for miles and the "inspectors" concluded many brick masons must have worked on the job at tremendous cost.

For years Aurora was a magnificent ghost town, intact except for some frame buildings lost by fire. But later the blocks of brick buildings, many still holding their contents, were wantonly razed for their bricks. Mrs. Ella Cain, who with her husband, owns most of Bodie and Aurora, told this author a few years ago: "We couldn't keep up the taxes on all those buildings and gave permission for removal of enough bricks to reduce the building valuations. Vandals came in and removed almost everything, entirely wrecking the town."

Today there are barely enough remains to give some vague outlines — foundations, shapeless piles of brick, an iron door. The streets can be seen though overgrown with sage brush. There is exactly one brick building intact and why that was left is a mystery.

"SCOTTY" McLEOD hauls first baby carriage to Rawhide in first rush of 1907. Note bale of hay, bed spring, barrel of flour, box of china and high chair. Of pair engaged in horse play, man at left is Charles B. Holman who named town Rawhide in fit of pique over rebuffs in self-sufficient camp of Buckskin.

RAWHIDE, NEVADA

"Rawhide was named by an early prospector who mended his worn out clothes with a strip of that material" . . . "The town was called by that name because some of the first ore was hauled out in raw cowhides" . . . "The first mail box was put up along the trail with a sign that read 'All mail for this camp here'. The box was nailed to a post which had a hide on it, tail still attached."

"All a pack of lies," says Charles A. McLeod. "I went into what is now Rawhide on Feb. 12, 1907 with Albert J. Bovard and prospected around that section and on Feb. 12 I made my first location on what is known as Hooligan Hill. My first claim was named Happy Day and the second Happy Hooligan. My partner Bovard went southwest to Pilot Peak, about four miles from our camp, but did not find anything. Charles B. Holman and my brother Mason arrived at our camp just a few hours after I had made my locations. I had left word at Schurz for them to follow Bovard and myself.

"Charley Holman was very bitter about his recent experience at Buckskin, a new boom camp not far away. They had told him they didn't want any more prospectors making claims around there. He was fuming about this all through supper and finally he exploded. "By God!" he said. "They think they're so darn smart getting that name of Buckskin on the map! We'll go them one better and get a Rawhide on it!' We always called the camp Rawhide after that, and that's what it was after others came in."

The man who relates this incident and other vivid and colorful ones is Charles McLeod who at 86 still makes visits to scattered claims in Rawhide and elsewhere, but living more quietly now in Yerington, Nevada. He is Scotty to his friends which

HERE WAS MAIN STREET of town. In background is Regent Range, composed of rock materials so light colored as to appear snow covered. Derelict buildings are survivors of fire which all but leveled Rawhide at height of inflated prosperity. Vegetation is sparse—dry, hot climate in summer and cold in winter hostile to most plants. Among few ornamental shrubs cultivated was Tamarisk, surviving example at left of small building left of center, still sending out airy panicles of pinkish bloom in spring.

FADED, DESERTED BUILDINGS on street leading to Hooligan Hill are silent only in rare periods of calm weather. When wind blows old structures come to ghostly sort of life, galvanized metal of roofs clanking loudly, metal barrels rolling noisily, loose boards flapping against walls, weeds gyrating wildly.

means everyone privileged to meet him and has a remarkable memory and keen wit. His birthplace was the early day camp of Aurora, Nevada and/or California — the town belonging to two states at one time. A boyhood spent in the never-ending clamor of hundreds of stamp mills and constant talk of assays and values conditioned Scotty to a life closely associated with mines and mining. Even before his family's stay at Aurora, his father owned a ranch at Yerington, the one-time Pizen Switch.

Here at the cross roads of travel west to the Sierra and north to Oregon, an opportunist once set a board on two whiskey kegs and peddled the contents to dusty-throated travelers. Business was brisk and as the whiskey level got low the resourceful samaritan fired up the raw stuff with tobacco juice

and what-have-you, adding water for bulk. So Pizen Switch the spot was, the place where the McLeods settled on the ranch. Other settlers rebelled at the name and called it Mason Valley and later the village took the name of Yerington which today is still a thriving farm center.

Aurora was fading fast when the McLeods left it but Charles had a boy's curiosity and touch of gold fever. Before he reached his majority he was prospecting around Mason Valley and at about twenty-five staked out the claims on Hooligan Hill a few hours before the camp was christened Rawhide.

That was in February, 1907. Ever restless, as soon as the claims were proved to be rich, he and Charley Holman sold out their joint properties of

some nineteen claims to Van Doren and Dunning for $20,000 plus 10% of profits. They went prospecting elsewhere but by fall the magnet of the booming Rawhide proved so strong they returned to start working the several claims retained at the north end of Stingaree Gulch. In the meantime Van Doren and Dunning had sold out to the Nat C. Goodwin Co. for $400,000, with McLeod and Holman still getting their 10%. Goodwin was a famous New York comedian enamored of western mining, his company incorporated for $3 million.

The landscape around Rawhide was undoubtedly as stark and barren, yet as fascinating, then as now. A small amount of grass and sagebrush grows along the sides of Stingaree Gulch which bisects the camp but otherwise the mountains, rising sharply on all sides, each of a different color, seem utterly unclothed. But the early inhabitants were likely unaware of such harsh beauty, busy as they were working their claims or prospecting.

Miners on Grutt Hill thought dynamite was necessary to follow a promising vein of gold. The head powder man had imbibed a few too many and placed the blasting material with too lavish a hand — which he was lucky not to lose. The resulting explosion startled the town but nobody was hurt, and a few even helped. The hoped for vein of rich ore was where it was expected to be — until the blast scattered it to Rawhide's far sides. The owners recovered about $14,000 but much was pulverized and lost, much picked up and pocketed by grateful citizens.

Another and less spectacular blast at the Coalition mine sent a chunk of ore through the window of the First National Bank of Rawhide. A bank official, able to "assay" the rock, deducted the value of it from window repair costs and returned a balance of $8 to the owners.

Not all the Rawhide ore was valued for its gold alone. Some material assayed out eight ounces of gold to one of silver, the next batch showing the same values in reverse. Some of the best left indications in the report of $26,000 to the ton. "And it was shallow, easy to get at," says Scotty. "Our claims at the north edge of town produced almost all their good ore between 35 and 94 feet, which was at bedrock."

Rawhide had its sharpies, hangers-on who didn't enjoy working in mines but made their living supplying workers with expensive pleasures of

RAWHIDE HOOSEGOW—most substantial building in town, Roaring waters of flood in Stingaree Gulch threatened foundations but did not undermine them. Part of stone walls caved but cells still held prisoners, roaring days of Rawhide's short prosperity furnishing good supply.

the flesh or extracting even more gold by mine stock manipulation. Rawhide did not seem to care about a man's previous reputation, was not even curious about it, as in the case of one of its more prominent citizens, George Graham Rice. He had done a very good job at promoting the L. M. Sullivan Trust Co. in Goldfield, so good that $10 million had poured into its owner's pockets, almost none in the stockholders'. The whole enterprise collapsed when these stockholders ganged up on President "Shanghai Larry" Sullivan who was thoroughly bewildered to find his erstwhile aide gone with the wind and a considerable chunk of the funds. But Rice hadn't gone far, only to Rawhide where he lost no time in setting up another operation. This was so successful he contracted for a magazine series at three cents a word. With neither caution nor modesty he titled the stories, "My Adventure With Your Money". The series attracted much attention, in-

STARK HOOLIGAN HILL looms behind town. Much scarred by diggings, it shows none of feverish activity in boom days. Stingaree Gulch, once notorious locale of extensive (some say 600 girls) red light district, lies just below hill in immediate foreground. Gulch also was scene of flood which swept away all flimsy shacks, leaving several inches of sand on floors of sturdier ones.

WONDER LUMBER CO. building is one of monuments to failure in town where many fortunes were made. Founder was soon called "Hard Luck Kenny" by sympathetic townsmen. Kenny had come fresh from fiasco in Portland, Oregon, where real estate venture failed. Scotty McLeod and Barker Butler staked him to have fling at mine which proved a dud. Unfortunate man met end on Black Desert when car broke down. Trying to repair engine, Kenny got gasoline on hands which ignited, burning him to death.

cluding that of federal investigators who eventually confined the activities of the promoter-author behind the discouraging bars of the federal penitentiary at Atlanta.

And there was Tex Rickard who also came over from Goldfield, attracted as others were away from the slightly frayed-at-edge camp to the new bonanza town whose star was blazing. Rickard had been operating his Goldfield Northern Saloon, in which he owned most of the stock, but liked excitement such as his fantastically successful promotion of the Joe Gans-Battling Nelson fight which brought some forty thousand people to Goldfield. His Northern Saloon had been built with money from the stake he made in the Klondike rush where he cut his teeth on the entertainment racket.

Now Goldfield was growing tiresome and Tex sold his interests to one Johnny Mays and staged a farewell party at the Northern. Feeling exuberant on his way to his Thomas Flyer he took cue chalk and scrawled on the door of an abandoned church— "This church closed. God has gone to Rawhide."

A better than average photographer, Scotty Mc-

Leod loved to record the scenes of his early mining days. One of his pictures shows the spot where he and his companions camped at what would later be Rawhide, their little white tent the only sign of habitation in the lonely desert landscape. When Rickard arrived about a year later he bought a lot next to this spot for his new Northern, paying $10,000.

At this time, the peak of prosperity in Rawhide's short but hectic life, the population was estimated at some five thousand. The camp had three banks which stayed open until midnight before there was an official post office. A large portion of a business block shows clearly in a 1909 photograph — the High Grade Bar, G and K Drug Store, Rawhide Clothing House, the Northern and Hermitage, another bar. Not shown are the other thirty-seven saloons and four churches. In addition the town boasted of a school, steam laundry, twenty-eight restaurants, the "Princess" theater, twelve hotels, telegraph and telephone lines. During the first year, it is reported, Sunday masses for Catholics were held in a saloon that closed just before dawn which gave the "church" time to clean up and carry in benches and a crude portable altar.

Then came Elinor Glyn. The lady had recently written the novel, "Three Weeks". Sufficient effort was made to suppress the sensational book to assure its popularity and Elinor G. was riding high. Rickard seized the moment to invite the lady to Rawhide to see how "the other side" lived. Mrs. Glyn accepted, possibly because Rickard had been clever enough to extend the invitation through Nat Goodwin, a friend of the now famous lady author and promoter in Rawhide. Perhaps Mrs. Glyn also saw a chance to gather some publicity while researching the seamy mining camp. She arrived by way of San Francisco with two friends, Sam Newhouse and Ray Baker. All were made welcome with every stunt the ingenious Rickard and Goodwin team could think of.

After several rounds of champagne in Rawhide's best hotel the party was escorted to a poker game in another room. The players were hired to ignore Mrs. Glyn and put on a good show for her, six shooters and all. An argument developed and the guns barked — at the ceiling. La Glyn and her friends beat a hasty retreat, tarrying outside long enough to listen for further gunfire. One horrified glance showed the "bodies" of two players being carried out.

Escorts of the Glyn Guided Tour paused only long enough to make sure she observed the stretcher bearers headed for the combination furniture-undertaker establishment, then proceeded down Stingaree Gulch. Most of the lower end of the Gulch bisecting the town was given over to cribs and the girls had been coached to make every effort to seduce Mrs. Glyn's friends.

At the far end of the street a shack was set afire, the blaze being soon extinguished by the Rawhide Volunteer Fire Department. The fire laddies made up in flashy uniforms and flourishes what the tiny pump cart and meager water supply lacked. That evening another fancy champagne dinner was served for the novelist and the next morning she and her friends left for the East properly impressed with the "innate aristocracy" of the miners of Nevada. Large bursts of publicity in national newspapers both for Mrs. Glyn and Rawhide, made everybody's efforts well worth while though many editors saw through the farce and said so.

On September first rumors came to the town of a rich strike at nearby Silver Lake and Scotty McLeod headed there with his cronies. He was gone just long enough to miss seeing the near total destruction of Rawhide. Three days after he left some-

one opened a window in a back room of the Rawhide Drug Store, the resulting stream of air blowing a curtain across a gasoline stove on which lunch was being prepared. In moments the room was ablaze and before the R.V.F.D. could get there flames were shooting from several stores. Jerry-built, tinder dry frame structures, they went up like match sticks and flung blazing brands on neighboring buildings and in a few hours nine blocks of the business district were leveled. Tex Rickard watched the flames devour his Northern Saloon, rushed to the telegraph office to order building material for a new one.

The gesture was brave but futile. Rawhide was never the same. Many stores were replaced on their old sites but business failed to get its strength back. The truth, painful as it became evident, was that Rawhide had existed more on promotion, flamboyancy and stock juggling than on the bona fide production of gold and silver. Values in these metals were there but not in sufficient quantities to justify the old, extravagantly-touted Rawhide. Mining by then in Nevada had passed its peak of glamor and as once prosperous businesses failed, ghosts moved in.

Rawhide today displays a large number of picturesque old false-fronted buildings, mostly those which escaped the fire. The ghost town fan who is willing to drive long distances over gravel roads will find atmosphere in abundance in Rawhide, an outstanding example of fast boom and quick bust, of flagrant over-promotion which ballooned it beyond reason, out of all chance for a less flashy but more permanent success.

TYPICAL OF PERIOD is pressed metal sheathing for face of building. This and galvanized roofing saved these structures from disastrous fire. At left was combination store and post office, former owned by Mr. and Mrs. Leonard, wife being postmistress for over twenty years.

BROKEN HILLS, NEVADA

Joseph Arthur just stood there staring. He could hardly believe in the reality of the gleaming rock there on the ground, glinting with bright streaks of metallic silver. When he picked it up and turned it over and over, he found he was talking to himself. "This is it! This is it!" And indeed the chunk of float proved to be a fair sample of the wealth soon unearthed in the sagebrush covered Broken Hills.

The discovery was not a haphazard stroke of luck. No burro's frisking heels uncovered it, nor any dying vulture's thrashing wings. It was the just reward of a long conducted search. In fact when Joe Arthur was only a small boy he had stood on a hill with his father who had brought him to Eastern Nevada. He looked out over the vast panorama to the west and asked: "What's over there, dad?" The answer: "Many ranges of mountains with many valleys between. That's where prospectors go looking for gold and silver." Little Joe considered that as he traced the outlines of the ranges sharply defined in the desert air. "That's what I'm going to do," he said with conviction, "when I grow up".

The Arthur family, father, mother, sister and Joe — had come to the new raw country from England. Mr. Arthur got a job in the Ruby mines and on Sundays preached in momentarily quiet saloons and gambling houses. As soon as Joe was old enough to work he too got a job in the mines, all the while listening to talk and reading about mining, metallurgy and prospecting for his own education. As soon as he could he headed out into the mountains — and learned a hard lesson. The first few years he met nothing but discouragement but he learned how to persevere. He kept on prospecting and working in the mines when he had to for money to keep on prospecting.

The gods were on his side for in the same vicinity another Englishman, James M. Stratford was looking for something better to happen. Stratford had made one fairly good strike in the Desatoyas, a few miles north of where the modern day town of Gabbs is. A moderate rush had poured in around the claim and a little town named for him. But the mineral wealth proved to be confined to his claim only and was very modest at that. So the camp melted away and left Stratford to eke out a meager living. Now Joe Arthur came along to check on a claim he had filed in the Stratford area. He found no metal but did find a kindred spirit in Jim Stratford. The two joined forces and that fall headed into the hills together.

They worked all winter and into spring, systematically pecking at ledges, cracking pieces of float, panning samples of gravel in streams. Results? Nothing but discouragement. On the evening of

STORES and other places of business in Broken Hills were modest, this one including living quarters at left. Storage shelter for food supplies is dugout, partly showing at rear corner.

GRAVE OF MATT COSTELLO is lonely one on top of knoll. After life of grinding poverty miner made good strike, sold claim for $1,500. Few days later he was found dead, sitting at his table. Friends buried him near cabin all traces of which have vanished.

April 12 as the two were preparing supper, Jim breathed his discontent. "I'd sure like a cup of coffee when it's ready. Joe — let's call it quits." We'll never find anything this way." Joe nodded — but he hadn't forgotten the lesson he'd learned, keep on trying. "Let's look around just one more day, Jim. If nothing shows up by tomorrow evening, I'll be ready to give up."

The next morning the men separated so as to cover as much ground as possible, Jim taking the ridge, Joe the gully. In the first half hour Joe found several small pieces of promising material and followed the trail, growing more excited by the

foot. He kept picking up more fragments until he saw the large, glittering rock.

He had been almost afraid to let himself believe the signs but now he let his feelings break loose and was shaking all over. As soon as he could get settled down he piled rocks to mark the outcropping from which his silvery find had come, then systematically staked out three claims — the Belmont, Grand Prize and Butler. With his own "grand prize" in his hands he went back to camp and waited anxiously. A pot of coffee was waiting for Jim when he returned dejectedly. "I didn't find a thing. How about you?" In dramatic silence Joe held out the silvery rock.

SMALL, SCRUBBY DESERT GROWTHS persisting in dry gravel cast long shadows as another long, lonely day ends for Broken Hills. Town's life was lively but short, only strike of value being that of man who founded town. Main street was curving gravel road at right. Facing buildings here are a few more across road.

Partners Arthur and Stratford were able to raise money for equipment and supplies to start operation by simply showing some of the ore so rich in gold and silver. Others flocked in, scraping away sagebrush to start a little one street town called Broken Hills. One of the men, Maury Stromer, long afterward told Nell Murbarger, author of "Ghosts of the Glory Trail"; "It was a nice little town, good, decent folks — decent and law abiding. Sure, we had a few saloons, bawdy houses and gambling halls, but they didn't dominate the place."

Joe and Jim stayed with it for five years by which time they had taken out $60,000. They then sold out to George Graham Rice, notorious promoter of Rawhide, for $75,000. Joseph Arthur, still only forty-three, retired to Reno to live with his wife Zua, and Stratford, ten years older, also retired.

In 1921 there was a substantial hotel in Broken Hills operated by partners Daniels and Ross of Yerington, Nevada. "Scotty" McLeod of the latter place tells of the tragedy that took place there. Ross had a beautiful daughter, an accomplished pianist. A single man was greatly attracted to her but the girl did not return his feelings. The man made strenuous advances one evening when they were alone in the kitchen. Repulsed, he raged out of the hotel, first emptying a kerosene lamp on the floor in the hallway and setting it on fire. Neither Daniels nor the girl's father was in the building and first learned of the disaster when they saw the flames. Ross tore himself from restraining arms, dashed into the inferno to find his daughter on her knees in a corner of the kitchen "with her hands folded as if she were praying."

Her father dragged her to the door where he collapsed. "His ears were burned clear off and the flesh fell from his hands," Scotty says. Ross soon died in agony and a double funeral was held in Yerington. "My wife and I went to both service and mass the next morning. It was the saddest thing we ever knew."

Broken Hills was a waterless place. Every drop had to be hauled several miles across the desert from Lodi Tanks, natural reservoirs. Lodi had been a booming camp in the '70s with hotel, saloons, etc. but it died early, leaving only the water. When Rawhide flared into lusty life in 1907, miners had a need for water though despising it for drinking purposes. So Lodi Tanks came to life again and had spurts of activity every time another camp sprang up. It was a spasmodic sort of existence but Lodi had nothing else. When Broken Hills came begging for water, Lodi was willing to provide it. It was free at the source but by the time it was hauled to Broken Hills by wagon it cost $2.50 a barrel. Later Maury Stromer obtained a truck and hauled the water for $1.

Arthur and Stratford left a 6,000 ton pile of inferior ore on their dump to be worked when and if a suitable mill was erected. It was this potential added to the mines that interested George Graham Rice. His interest was not quite the same as the original owners. He was a promoter only, his methods in Goldfield and later Rawhide only a bare jump ahead of the law. Before he acquired the Arthur-Stratford mine he sent geologist Arthur Perry Thompson to check out the possible wealth in Broken Hills at $60 a day. This was to appear in a fancy prospectus and sometimes a geologist at $60 a day could make things appear very glossy. Sure enough the reports from Broken Hills were very enthusiastic. Cracker Jack, Black Dog, Grand Prize, Belmont, Go-Between and the Broken Hills claims were all of "unusual merit, fully deserving of future development". Governor Emmett D. Boyle, himself a veteran mining man, also seemed to see a rosy future for the camp — "The best potential I've seen in any new Nevada territory for many years." Analyzed, the ambiguous statements did not mean the prospects were good but who wanted to doubt anything that sounded like they wanted it to sound. Much property changed hands and the Arthur and Stratford holdings were paid for by Rice — with, of course, his stockholders' money.

As it happened the new owners of the claims could not get going, though now and then they did send in a small shipment of reasonably good ore, enough to keep the share holders from screaming too loudly. Altogether production under the new management amounted to a paltry 35 tons worth some $7,000. When some investors compared this with the $75,000 dropped in the mine shafts, they put the glasses on Mr. Rice. His activities led to a full scale investigation and his confinement in the penitentiary.

Smaller operators took over at Broken Hills, the town barely existing. There was a minor burst of activity during the depression years and figures show a production of $197,195 between 1935 and 1940. As people returned to their former jobs, Broken Hills faded away entirely, except for Maury Stromer. He continued to work his mine, the Badger, the hard way, descending to dig ore, loading it in the bucket, hauling it back up. He made about $5 a day at this backbreaking work.

Winters are raw with snow in Broken Hills and Maury finally took some holidays with his daughter in Paso Robles, California. He was taken ill in March, 1956, and died in the hospital. Burial was in his beloved Nevada at Reno. That left Broken Hills, a place deserted except for jackrabbits bounding among the sagebrush and pack rats making homes in the empty shacks.

"HIS" AND "HERS", built straddling worthless mine shaft, offering some hazards as supports barely touch crumbling edges of deep hole. Incidental is beauty of desert —etched wood showing grains and textures.

ARIZONA

STANTON, ARIZONA

"From Monastery To Murder" could have been the title of a biography of Charles P. Stanton if he could have found anybody to write it. By one means or another, always devious, he got what he wanted which was to be "king of the camp" and was the most hated and feared man in the Antelope Valley.

Stanton began his adult life in an atmosphere of rectitude as novice in a monastery but was soon expelled on charges of immorality. Drifting west he passed in and out of many mining camps, always learning some new way of making a "fast buck", preferably by latching on to some innocent's hard-earned cash. Then he struck the Antelope Valley and saw opportunity with a big "O".

The Rich Hill district with the Congress, Weaver, Antelope and Octave mines in Antelope Valley, was one of the several productive placer areas discovered by the Pauline Weaver party in the early 1860's. When the stage line through the Valley established a regular stop there, the place took the name of Antelope Station. The usual saloons, boarding houses and stores grew up along the placer beds, centering around the general store of the popular partners, Wilson and Timmerman.

In Antelope Station Stanton settled in a small cabin near the partners' store. His first intention may have been to pan some of the easy gold in the creek but if so the noble desire was short lived. More to his liking was the Wilson and Timmerman business.

He started a well-planned, three-way plot, pitting the partners against another Antelope resident, William Partridge. Hate was worked up between Partridge and Wilson, then Stanton slipped the word that Wilson was out gunning for the other. Partridge flared up, took the initiative and shot the merchant in the street in true Western style. Partridge was convicted of a murder and sent to the penitentiary largely because of adverse testimony by his supposed friend, Charles P. Stanton.

Smugly, he now began to lay plans to shorten the future of partner Timmerman. Sure enough the man was found dead one day, a coroner's jury unable to say whether the death was suicide from grief over his partner's passing or simply an accident.

Up to now Stanton had not been suspected but when he took over the store and claimed the partners had left it to him, people began to wonder. After a continuing series of mysterious acts of violence, all happening to those who stood in Stanton's way, suspicion became certainty. But his power and influence was so great no one dared to lift a voice— no one except Barney Martin who was heard on several occasions to say: "Something should be done about Charles Stanton."

Then one midnight a stranger knocked at Martin's door and gave warning. "A lot of strange things have been happening in this town, what with people getting killed and all. Get your family out of here before they are all murdered."

OLD CONGRESS HOTEL is still in use as private residence. Giant saguaro cacti were planted as small seedlings when town and hotel were flourishing. Holes in upper areas made by woodpeckers as nests are often occupied later by elfin owls. Cactus plant forms hard, air- and water-tight linings around pockets, once used by Indians for water bags. When photographer set up tripod in yard it was filled with milk goats, all scampering out except one curious maverick.

Martin was no personal coward but he knew he couldn't keep guard over his family the clock around. So he sent a man on horseback to tell his friend Captain Calderwood that his family would be arriving at Calderwood Station in a day or two, then he piled his family into a wagon and left town.

Linked with Stanton's nefarious interests were the Valenzuela brothers who were to come up short in the holdup at the Vulture mine. These two desperadoes in company with several others followed the Martin wagon and forced it off the road after it was well away from the camp. The entire family was then murdered, dry brush piled on the wagon and the whole set on fire. When the Martins failed to appear at Calderwood, the captain sent out a search party which traced the wagon tracks to the scene of carnage.

Yet nothing was done to check Stanton's supremacy for fear of reprisal. Instead of suffering

for his misdeeds he now took over the whole town, even changing its name to his own. Feeling secure as "king of the camp", Stanton began pressing his attentions on a beautiful Mexican girl, Froilana, daughter of Pedro Lucero who was leader of a gang of toughs in neighboring Weaver. The girl had different ideas and no intention of submitting to him. Stanton, not used to resistence in any form, forced the issue. The next day in his store, he turned to face what he thought was a customer and quickly saw it was the girl's brother Jose. Before Stanton could draw his gun, Jose put two .44 slugs into the chest of the man who had wronged his sister.

Fleeing from the scene, young Lucero met a friend coming down the trail who inquired the reason for all the hurry. "I have just killed Stanton," he replied, "and I am hurry up to get across the border." The friend caught his arm. "Wait. Don't go. We will get up a reward for you."

OLD STAGE STATION and depot in what was first called Antelope Valley, later Stanton. At left of structure is long line of sleeping rooms for travelers.

"HOME COMFORT" CLASSIC for travelers at Stanton's stage depot. Meat was fairly plentiful, mostly pork raised by residents, fresh fruits and vegetables almost non-existent. When beef was not shipped in, hunters shot antelope.

DESERTED STORE BUILDINGS offer ideal conception of ghost town. Scene is in Congress Junction, often just Congress, at point where dirt road comes down from Stanton, Weaver and Octave, old gold towns in fringes of Bradshaw Mountains. At first Congress was only supply depot for earlier camps, then rich mine was discovered nearby, the Dennis May, which became Arizona's deepest gold diggings. Later owner was picturesque "Diamond Joe" Reynolds who had owned string of steamboats on Mississippi, company called Diamond Joe. With no mill at mine ore was shipped to Prescott on "twenty mule schooners". Small building at right was post office about which was said: "The present Congress post office was not there before same post office that was in existence prior to 1938 but rather is the same post office that was formerly known as Congress Junction." QED

WEAVER, ARIZONA

Pauline Weaver was Tennessee born in 1800, the father a white man, mother the daughter of an Indian chief. Pauline was destined to be honored by having the name Weaver used for a mining camp, not because Pauline was some girl wonder of Arizona but because *he* was a military scout and public benefactor. The Indian mother named her baby Paulino which became Pauline in usage. Although a strange sounding name for a rugged character, it was not an uncommon one among half-breeds. Weaver however was to distinguish himself from the ordinary.

The boy started his wandering career as soon as he cut loose from his mother's buckskin "apron strings", ranging from home to Puget Sound and into Arizona. On the great ruin of Casa Grande one can see written on the walls: "Pauline Weaver was here — 1832" but he cannot be blamed for desecration. Pauline could not read or write.

In 1847 General Stephen W. Kearny hired him as military guide to lead the Mormon Battalion from New Mexico to California, rewarding him with a land grant in the area of present Banning. But the man was not a farmer and headed back to Arizona. In common with other "mountain men" he carried several weapons — his long-barreled, muzzle-loading flintlock gun, later a percussion cap type, then there was his bowie-type knife for skinning, butchering and eating.

While many of these men traveled in bands for safety. Weaver, like Bill Williams, preferred going it alone. One memorable exception was his gathering a party including Major A. H. Peeples, Jack Swilling, several other whites and some Mexicans. They were at La Paz after the discovery of gold there but came late and were not satisfied with what they found, pushing on through the arid desert region toward the Bradshaw Mountains. They reached a good stream of water, shot several antelope and made camp. The stream was named Weaver Creek in honor of the guide and the location Antelope Valley. This spot later became Stanton.

Next morning the horses were missing and the Mexican aides were sent after them. Covering the high hill nearby and beyond it, they not only found the animals but an abundance of *chispas*, nuggets the size of pebbles. Gathering a handful, they returned with the horses and told their story. Without waiting for breakfast, Major Peeples rushed over the mountain shoulder and picked up $7,000 in gold before returning to camp.

History says the men soon cleaned up the surface deposits but neglects to state if they ever had

FOUNDATIONS FOR MILL BUILDINGS in Weaver contain much native rock, not much scarce cement. Little adobe structure, center background, is typical of area where lumber was unobtainable. Formerly roofed with brush and mud, new mining activity at turn of century saw sheet metal roof as replacement, and even this has suffered from ravages of time. Building served as store, is lone survivor of business section of once flourishing camp, now only waste of rubble and brush. Tiny cemetery has no headboards standing now but in 1918 thirty-five were counted, all bearing legends: "Died with his boots on."

STONE POWDER HOUSE barely retains heavy iron door. Site is immediately below Weaver, likely chosen as safe distance. Large saguaro cactus may easily be several hundred years old and weigh several tons, is supported vertically by heavy woody-fibered structure, rest is pulp composed mostly of water. Rock intrusion in background is home for countless rattlesnakes, area known as "Rattlesnake Haven."

breakfast. As soon as the news got out a horde of whites and Mexicans burst on the scene in a full-scale gold rush. The mountain became known as Rich Hill, the mushrooming collection of adobes as Weaver Camp, later Weaverville, then Weaver. As men swarmed in, each claim was limited to 200 square feet and claim jumping was common.

When the camp's short life came to an end, the placers alone had given up a total of $1 million and lodes were found both at Weaver and the neighboring camp of Octave. The latter was appropriately named as eight partners found deposits.

Not having a miner's temperament, Weaver departed quickly. In 1867 he was again hired as a guide and attached to Camp Lincoln, later Camp Verde. Refusing a bunk in the barracks he occupied a tent outside the reservation. On the morning of June 21, a soldier was sent to see why the guide had not reported as scheduled and found Weaver dead in the tent. Everything was neatly in order

and the body wrapped in a blanket. Weaver had apparently been sharing the tent with an Apache and a year or so before had received an arrow in the shoulder. The shaft was removed but the head remained and this was thought to have caused his death.

He was buried with military honors by the companies of the 14th Regiment stationed at Camp Lincoln in the cemetery there. In 1892, after the Indian scares had subsided, remains of all military personnel including those of Weaver, were removed to San Francisco yet Weaver was not to rest there but to be a wanderer in death as he had been in life. In 1928 a movement was started in Prescott to bring the remains to the spot where in 1863 he had made as permanent a camp as he ever did. The spot is on the grounds of the Sharlot Hall Museum in Prescott, and is marked by a large stone bearing a bronze plate inscribed: "PAULINE WEAVER — truly a great man."

COMBINATION STONE and dugout buildings served as business section in better days of large gold mining camp of Octave, close neighbor of Weaver. In 1863 rich gold placer beds were discovered in Weaver Creek by party of eight men to commemorate their number.

MILL AT OCTAVE was built in expectation of many years of production by quartz veins, which were exhausted by end of century. Even so, Octave mine, consisting of two shafts 1,300 feet deep, turned out more than $8 million.

McCABE, ARIZONA

McCabe, the Bradshaw Mountains, had its deep-well mystery but there is no cloud of uncertainty about its final demise. And it did not deserve such a fate. It was a family town, suffering a stroke when the gold faded out, was then inundated by an angry flood.

When gold was found in the creek in the late 1860s, there was a rush to get in on the first easy placerings, after which the town was almost deserted until the mother lode was located. A more permanent town then grew up as hard rock mining progressed with several deep shafts bored and a number of stamp mills erected. A two-story brick building on a gentle rise above the creek bed was the largest and most impressive in town. It housed a large general store and several smaller businesses.

Most of the miners were married and as a family town McCabe did not have the usual shootings and scrapes of early Western camps. One old timer described conditions as "dull". "Oh, there was always the hell-raising town of Providence. It was barely over the hill and within easy walking distance. A man could get anything he might want there and some things he didn't, like a broken nose or a slug of hot lead." But McCabe virtuously preserved its reputation as a "clean town."

A good-sized school house stood just above the store and across the road. On the summit of the hill was the immense building housing all the company offices with refinements not found in most camps, including a granite fireplace, showers and flush toilets. A concrete water tank, perhaps two hundred feet across, was built just below the building yet high enough to supply the town by gravity. The water was not palatable because of heavy mineral content and drinking water was hauled up to the town by mule team, one driver in early days a Mr. Conley, helped by his son Earl.

A Swedish miner, Oscar Johnson, was the principal in McCabe's mystery. A loner, Johnson seemed to be doing very well at his claim. He was a hard worker, rising early as smoke could be seen coming from his shack on the north bank of the creek, and almost furtively, said curious observers, Oscar would emerge and head for his well. He had dug it himself, saying the water hauled into camp was too expensive, but the suspicious watchers remembered he had spent an inordinately long time at the digging, that he had removed far more dirt than the comparatively high water table would require.

The morning visits to the well, when Oscar would draw up a full bucket, seemed innocent

UNIQUE MONUMENT stands securely in cemetery on right side of difficult dirt road — first indication that there are traces of McCabe. Burial ground is deeply eroded by run-off waters, some graves washed entirely away. Monument is cast in one piece from some zinc-like metal, rings when rapped with knuckles. Placed in 1906, marker has enduring qualities but may overturn when foundation breaks down.

LIKE A MONUMENT to past mining glory, granite ruin of elaborate fireplace stands at summit above McCabe. On site stood large office buildings of mining company. Not far away is evidence of showers, granite floor area having drainage hole. Close by are shattered fragments of porcelain flush toilet, a mining camp rarity. Water was available from huge storage tank, circular basin some two hundred feet across. This was for domestic use and mill operations only, drinking water hauled in from stream.

enough, but there were those frequent night trips too, with a lantern. Unable to stand the suspense, one man stationed himself behind a bushy manzanita and waited. After dark Johnson emerged from the cabin with a ladder and a lantern, taking them to the well then returning for a heavy bag. He lifted the well cover and let down the ladder,

OLD SAFE near general store appears to have been blown open. Resting on bed of clean gravel, surrounded by manzanita chaparral, it gives no further clues of violence.

descending with lantern and bag. The watcher waited for a long time it seemed until the miner came up, pulled up the ladder and went to the cabin. Rumor was quick to say Oscar Johnson was hoarding his wealth in the well but the incident was more or less passed by as just another peculiar trait of the recluse.

Then one day someone asked: "Say, where is Oscar Johnson? There hasn't been any smoke coming from his chimney for days." On a Sunday morning several men went to the cabin, found no Oscar Johnson but evidence he had not been there for several days. When a week went by and the man did not put in an appearance, a party investigated the well and reported there was a side tunnel about six feet down. With a lantern a man explored the tunnel and found a large room which showed every evidence of recent use but was entirely empty. Had Oscar been murdered and his wealth stolen? There was no sign of violence at the cabin or around his workings. No answer came. The industrious and secretive Scandinavian was never seen again, the mystery never solved.

One day in the late summer of 1937 black clouds gathered over the Bradshaws. It was the season for

BACKHOUSE was built of scarce lumber, is only frame structure in Leland, small mining community near McCabe.

rain, Arizona's mountain areas getting an annual fall of 25 to 30 inches in fall and winter. But this storm was heavier than most, the deluge concentrated in the several canyons that fed the stream pouring down through McCabe. As the waters rose in their narrow channel, some of the bulkheads against the rocky walls began to give way, timbering being carried far down the stream. As dirt and rock caved in, a temporary dam was formed and when the torrent built up enough pressure, it washed out the barrier and a huge wave came down on the town, brushing aside all buildings. No one was hurt, for no one was there and the damage was not known for months. McCabe was a ghost town and had been for years.

When the waters subsided, many buildings on higher ground still stood. The general store with stout brick walls was almost intact, the shed at the rear still housing a fabulous collection of buggies

from earlier days. Groceries and valuable merchandise had been hauled away before the flood but shelves of faded, outdated goods still remained. The school house stood on the rise across the street, blackboard walls still bearing chalked problems and grammar lessons.

Since then time, storm, decay and vandalism have taken their inevitable toll. The general store has been leveled, safe falling into the hole that was the cellar. The school was wrecked for lumber which was hauled down to Humboldt. There are even now a few shacks and many ruins showing where mills and a brick kiln once stood. On the side of one hill above the stream bed is a row of large settling tanks. Another larger tank, excavated from native rock and lined with concrete is high on the opposite side of the gulch and above is all that remains of the office buildings, the ruin of a big granite fireplace. This is the lonely lair of a ghost.

NEARBY LELAND CLAIM shows remains of much elaborate stone work. Large oak tree seems to guard enclosed well still holding water.

CLEATOR, ARIZONA

The story of Cleator, the town, is the story of Cleator, the man. It was his enterprise that built it and his right to sell it. You could have bought it in 1947 and it is there today to see.

James Patrick Cleator was born June 12, 1870, in Dhoon, Machold Parrish, on the Isle of Man in the Irish Sea. He went to school for a time but later admitted he "knew it all" when he reached the sixth grade. At 12 he went to sea as a cabin boy on the fishing boats and at 15 he was in the crews of grimy coal boats plying the coast from Newcastle to London. After working in a Thames River shipyard for several months he signed on, at 16, as able seaman on a ship hauling iron from Spain.

In 1887 young Cleator was a hand on the clipper ship *Arthur Stone* making a voyage around the Horn to Chile, loading nitrates there for San Francisco and flour there for Ireland. Now he was 19 and Jimmie knew the salty sea was not for him but the New World was. As a passenger he took ship to Halifax, train to Winnipeg and worked his way by odd jobs to San Francisco.

There was gold talk in the air and the erstwhile sailor turned to prospecting, finding a gold claim in California in 1898 and selling it for $10,000. Then he headed for Mexico, Chihuahua Province where he found nothing interesting and prospected various sections of Arizona. Attracted to British

OVER ALL VIEW OF CLEATOR—Town is placed in desert country at foot of pine-clad Bradshaws. Highest peak, Mount Wasson, over 8,000 feet, is in background. In center is original store and saloon. Left, nearer foreground, is stone schoolhouse built in WPA days. Original two-room schoolhouse is now home and rock shop of Phil and Audrey Reasoner. Desert growth is abundant, **Opuntia**, known as prickly pear, seen in clumps everywhere. Plant in left foreground is **Yucca**, bearing spikes of beautiful white flowers resembling lilies to which it is related. Author's camper is accidently left in photo.

ONE OF MANY STONE CABINS in hills behind Cleator. Primitive structure is typical of many shelters built of available material before lumber came in. Spiky plant in foreground is **Agave,** each leaf normally armed with stout, extremely sharp spike. Some have been trimmed off as plant has encroached on trail, wounding passers by.

Columbia he found the placers along the rivers long exhausted, so returned to the country he liked best, Arizona. Cleator found the Bradshaw Mountains to his liking and remained among them the rest of his life.

In 1902 a railroad was being built from Mayer to the area near the summit of Mount Wasson in the pine-covered Bradshaws where the fabulous Crowned King mine was being exploited. In the foothills the railroad passed the big Golden Turkey mine named for the many wild turkeys in the state. At the point of convenient access to this mine the rail line established loading platforms called Tur-

key Siding. A considerable crew of men was required to handle freight from and equipment to the Golden Turkey and several other mines along Turkey Creek. Some of the men were stationed there permanently, shacks and bunkhouses being built for them. One "Lev" Nellis set up a saloon and added a store beside it.

On New Year's Day, 1905, James Patrick Cleator walked into the saloon, had a drink and struck up conversation with Nellis. The two men found much in common and before the day was over formed a partnership, Cleator buying half-ownership. Lev had always wanted to raise cattle,

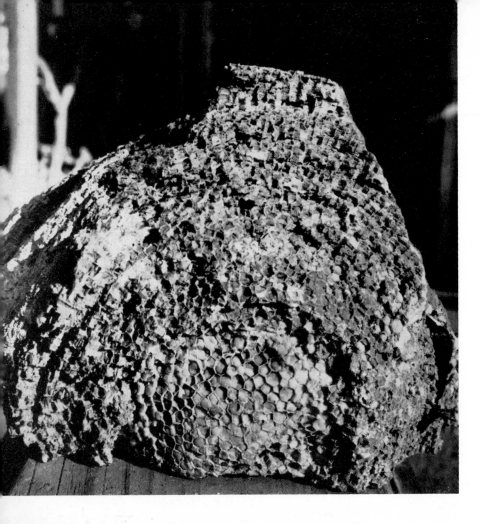

STRANGE "ROCK" is owned by Phil and Audrey Reasoner of Cleator. Object seems to be petrified hornet's nest which it strongly resembles in size, form, even color. Phil Reasoner mined in most of shafts and tunnels of New Mexico and Arizona, was forced to retire from effects of long continued breathing of dust from broken and crushed ore. He and wife now run interesting rock shop in Cleator.

had been too busy with the merchandising but now, with amiable and well-liked Cleator to run the store and saloon, he could turn most of his attention to the small herd he already owned.

In ten years both branches of the business had flourished to the point that both partners decided to separate, each taking over his favorite operation. By this time the settlement had grown to need a post office. Although known as Turkey Siding, the word "turkey" was in common use in the area, a new post office at Turkey Creek not far away. Cleator applied for a post office at his store and authorities gave it his name.

With the mines going well, Cleator also prospered as a supply base for them and its principal citizen took advantage of the situation to include real estate in his business. He built a number of small houses, renting and selling them. In all of them he installed the newfangled element—electricity—and piped in clear spring water. Cleator is in the desert but close to the high Bradshaws where rainfall is abundant.

At 77, James Cleator made a decision. He had been married years before to Pearl Hunt, the couple having a son and daughter. Now he would retire. Accordingly he advertised his town for sale, lock, stock and barrel, in the ARIZONA REPUBLIC. Other newspapers over the country caught the romance of the town for sale idea, repeating the ad with stories of the colorful life of James Patrick Cleator. A flood of letters came in, sometimes as many as fifty a day, but few of the curious wanted to buy a town and no sale was consummated. One newspaper reporter asked what he would like to do if he found a buyer. "I'd fix up an auto rig," Cleator answered, "and see the country."

The ruddy old gentleman died at 85 without fulfilling this wish. His widow, who also reached 85 in January of 1964, still lives in the town her husband built, retaining a keen memory for names, dates and events.

CROWN KING, ARIZONA

Just how was an army officer going to take time to work a gold claim? Maybe somebody smarter than he was had an easy answer but prospector A. F. Place, now an officer stationed at Fort Whipple, couldn't see one. The claim on the slopes of Mount Wasson in Arizona's Bradshaw Mountains did not offer too much but Place had to work it to keep it.

With some diligence he found an idle prospector, provided him with shovels, drilling and blasting tools and against his better judgment, paid him in advance. The man started for the claim through Tiger Camp, later Bradshaw City, and spotted a saloon where the doors seemed always to swing in. So he delegated his assignment and tools to two bull whackers and proceeded to relax.

The pair set to work on the claim and soon got down to hard rock. "Well, I guess it's about time you shot a hole," said one. The other looked blank. "Hell, I though you were the dynamite expert. I couldn't drill a hole let alone load it."

Falling back on the shovels they put in time on one spot and another. Toward evening they gathered up a few pieces of rock and walked back to the Tiger saloon where they found the prospector thoroughly mellow. "Nothing but these here pirates", the bull whackers reported." Jumping out of the fog, the prospector whooped: "Pyrites, hell — that's gold!" Such was the first discovery in the district and others would be richer.

Newspapers of that day gave such news full play and one of Prescott's flung banner lines across its pages, February 6, 1899: "The Richest Strike In The History Of Arizona!" and almost as heavy headlines followed: "Ore that runs $180,000 to the ton." Another mine in the Bradshaws was covered in the next line, only a little less black: "The Riches of The Peck Pale Before The Wealth In The Crowned King Mine!"

This splatter of ink stemmed from a letter written by Lester Jackson of the nearby War Eagle mine, just north of the Crowned King property. Jackson had descended the shaft to the 500-foot level, taken a "grab sample" and the assay had re-

vealed the fabulous values. The newspaper article quieted down to continue: "Mr. Jackson states that the sample was taken from a 10-inch chute of ore. He does not state the extent of the chute. Much excitement prevails all through the Bradshaws over the strike which is the greatest bona fide find in the history of Western quartz mining."

The paper's glowing reports failed to state the difficulty encountered with much of Crowned King ore. From the very first mills had trouble extracting the gold which assays showed was there. The first samplings of ore sent down by burro to the mills by the river proved so obdurate that run-of-the-mine ore was refused, mills accepting only less refractory material. Since burro-back transportation was expensive and slow, much ore was cast aside on the dumps. Later a railroad angled down the mountain as steeply as possible to where the wheels lost traction, then went through a series of switchbacks with the little train reversing itself on every hairpin turn.

By this time ore was being taken out at deeper levels and was improving in quality. Yet much of it

PHIL ANDREWS REVISITS MILL and assay office where he worked thirty-five years ago, was never able to recover gold values in ore discarded long ago as refractory. Scene is in Bradshaw Mountains named for David Bradshaw, pioneer who came to area from California where as member of Bear Flag party he was instrumental in capturing Sonoma, California, in 1846. Bradshaws at these higher levels are covered with dense timber, mostly pine.

ANDERSON'S SALOON, wild rendezvous of miners and prospectors in uninhibited early days of Crown King. Downstairs had large dance floor with bar at right, upper floor having central hallway with rooms for dance hall girls. Saloon had tamed down in days of town's rebirth when attempts were made to recover gold in dumps, but to Phil Andrews and other young, single men saloon was "off limits."

was still being thrown aside as too hard to mill. From time to time mining experts would cast covetous eyes at Crowned King ore but even as more modern methods of recovery came into use a big proportion was rejected either at mine or mill. While usage was shortening its name to Crown King piles of "good ore" remained on the dumps and became a legend into modern times. These were the times of Phil Andrews.

Having just graduated from college with a degree in chemistry, Stanley Phillips Andrews was ready for a career. One of his closest friends in San Diego in 1928 was Arthur Kipp, whose father was a mining engineer and friend of the senior Stanley Phillips Andrews. Young Phil was approached by Foster Kipp to take the job of laboratory technician and assistant in the assay office at the Crown King mine. The properties had been closed and abandoned for many years but the dumps of valuable ores were still tempting and Kipp thought he had figured out ways and means of converting them into money. He had backers ready to invest in a quarter million dollar mill at the site, another quarter mil-

lion in equipment and men to work over the old dumps. Previous assays of it ranged from $520 to $540 a ton and now it was estimated there were two and a half million dollars in the dump which could be worked profitably.

Of course the road was a hazard. Years before the railroad had been taken out and an automobile road built over the grade which had some comparatively gentle curves but the same precarious hairpin turns where the switchbacks had been. But it was the old trestles that raised the back hair. Planks were laid on these, barely wide enough for tires of cars which were Model Ts and later Model As. The spindly trestles that spanned deep canyons were but one car width, one of them having a sharp curve in the center, a driver honking his horn vigorously before venturing onto the span. All materials for the

CORNER OF DANCE HALL, Anderson's Saloon. Pancho Villa "got his start" as woodchopper at Crown King mine. When winter snows were deep and wood inaccessible, inveterate poker player Villa sought this cozy spot near stove.

"Y.M.C.A.," dormitory for younger members of crew during reactivation of town, was close to one of many exploratory shafts, or "gopher holes." Little structure about to collapse into cavity. Phil Andrews says of his residency here: "One of the boys was a fresh air fiend, would put his bed out on the porch (now gone), never went to the dances. When we returned from these affairs we had to climb over him to get in. He complained bitterly about being awakened."

new mill had to be hauled over these death-defying spans.

When Phil Andrews arrived for work he found about fifty people in the reactivated town. He had dinner at the fixed-up mess hall and bunked with several other young fellows in a small frame and sheet metal shack dubbed the "Y.M.C.A." The rest of the crew were all married.

Although actual assay work was new to him the process was familiar and he soon mastered the art of "bucking down" a batch of hard ore on the block, to "quarter" it again and again with a frame with two metal dividers to obtain a "quantitative analysis" by saving one quarter in each operation and discarding the rest. The weight of the sample saved was carefully compared with that of the shining silver and gold "button" which resulted from roasting the powdered ore, giving the values per ton.

Silver and gold could be separated for exact measuring.

Life after work was somewhat dull except for Saturday nights in the town where Phil and the other single fellows found a preponderance of girls, as most boys old enough to leave home were at jobs in Phoenix or away at school. There was a weekly dance in the old schoolhouse that attracted the local young people and ranchers from "below" who drove twenty miles or more even over the hair-raising trestles. The school desks would be moved against the wall, floor dusted with wax and Victrola started. There would be "Two Black Crows" and "Yes, We Have No Bananas" until things got going then waltzes and fox trots until the small hours — a family affair rather than a wild west or mining camp dance, everybody having a good time without too much drinking. It could be a man thought he

STAIRS USED BY MALE CUSTOMERS of girls in Anderson's Saloon. No girls now — hardly any stairs.

KITCHEN OF MESS HALL, now in complete ruin, was presided over by old Chinaman known simply as Yee. He had worked in California's Mother Lode, having shipped from China as cabin boy. Yee liked to do little things for friends, such as making cookies for Mrs. Kipp, manager's wife. She shared them with other ladies who clamored in vain for recipe. Knowing Phil was Yee's "pet," they asked him to get it. Formula resolved was: "Put in flour, put in sugar, put in butter, mix um up." Pressed for exact quantities, Yee was more explicit. "If make lots cookies, put in lots stuff." Feeling more expansive he told them how to shape cookies. "Put piece in hand, pat, pat, pat." Meat cooler was in dugout vault in background.

needed a clear head for driving on a road that included two planks on a spidery trestle over a deep canyon.

But things were not going well at the mill. Although Phil Andrews' assays continued to show the same good values, "we just weren't recovering," he says. "The values weren't going into the tailings either and we never did find out why the gold didn't show in the concentrates." The absentee backers be-

RAILROAD TIES formed walls of cabin. When narrow gauge railroad track to camp was taken up ties were used for houses. Crown King has left many solid remnants of early days in contrast to nearby Bradshaw City which has faded to slight outlines of stone foundations, is remembered most vividly for tragedy when mine car dropped full length of shaft killing seven miners.

LITTLE ONE ROOM SCHOOL still serves, teaching children of "summer resorters" who stay in mountains all winter. Ten pupils represent all grades except, as teacher Lorena Roberts explained: "Our fourth grade is home sick and our eighth grade is late getting back from lunch." Desks are same as those pushed back for dances long ago.

gan to think something was wrong and made a series of changes. Foster Kipp was discharged, Tomlinson had a chance to try his method and when nothing came of this, Earl Cranz was made manager and he tried his method which also failed. At this point the entire crew was let out and the operation ended.

Later other companies, or perhaps the same one, tried to extract Crown King's stubborn gold. One possibly had some success, as evidenced by a considerable pile of tailings, but at least three-fourths of the dump remains intact. When the WPB stopped gold mining in 1942 all further attempts at conversion were also stopped. Crown King today is occupied sparsely by a new non-mining group of summer visitors. The mountain refuge is a pleasant spot being about seven thousand feet high, cool in summer and shaded by whispering pines.

OF MUSTACHES AND MEN — Picture of miners was made at height of Crown King's prosperity, men working in largest mine, the Crown King. They were the steady customers at Anderson's Saloon and of the "frail sisters" upstairs. (Photo courtesy Sharlot Hall Museum, Prescott.)

BUMBLE BEE, ARIZONA

The prospectors were evidently more impressed with bumble bees than with Mr. Snyder for they changed the name of the settlement from Snyder's Station to Bumble Bee. Or it is possible they stumbled into bumble bee nests or as another story has it, they found Indians "as thick as bumble bees".

When W. W. Snyder settled in the valley there was plenty of water in the creek the year around with lots of lush pasture for his horses and cattle. There was also a crude road that penetrated the wild, "Indian infested" land. The term was Snyder's and the other whites', for of course the Indians were marauders for trying to drive the invaders from the Indian lands. And they were making some success of it when a small detachment of U.S. soldiers was sent into the valley to protect Snyder and other ranchers and prospectors to the good soil and water.

A stage line soon began irregular service and Snyder built a small hostelry and stable to accommodate travelers. The stop was known as Snyder's Station for many years. When gold was discovered in the adjacent Bradshaw Mountains, prospectors were soon dipping their pans in the creek.

Most gold discoveries were not made at Bumble Bee itself but in neighboring camps such as those along Turkey Creek — Golden Turkey, Cleator, Gloriana, the enormously rich Tip Top above Gillette, the Silver Prince, Black Warrior, Cougar, New Jersey and many more famous mines along the southwestern fringes of the Bradshaws. The Peck was outstanding. The first ten tons from that mine were sold to Prescott merchants for $10,000, so an old Prescott newspaper stated. Since the stage road to these areas led through Bumble Bee, the town shared a little of the prosperity.

Bumble Bee had gold of its own but the deposits were so rich a man could get no more than a little section the size of a blanket — hence a "blanket claim". From even this small area he might make $100 a day, for a few days. Some of the gravel beds large enough and lasting long enough to acquire names and an illusory fame were Chinese Bar, Portuguese Bar and the Dead Man. Even these were practically exhausted by the early 1900s and remained dormant until depression years when desperate men combed the sands for a few flakes of gold.

All through the years the town has tried to stay "by the side of the road", moving to follow survey realignments three times. At last it was by-passed so far by the Black Canyon highway it could not follow, now remains complacent on a good graveled side road.

PRESENT TOWN OF BUMBLE BEE was offered for sale in eastern newspapers, was purchased lock, stock and barrel by magazine publisher Charles E. Penn and wife Helen, who have restored it to original form.

SPECIMEN OF BUCKHORN or Staghorn Cholla, **Opuntia Acanthacarpa,** seen against light of low November sun. Traveler descending from Bradshaw Mountains where pine and oak trees predominate, soon feels he is in Arizona again as distinctive cacti are encountered in Bumble Bee area where Sonoran desert type of vegetation prevails. Beautiful Buckhorn plant is treacherous, slightest touch dislodging joints which break off and fasten themselves by barbed spines to human or animal flesh. Stems lying horizontally on ground quickly send roots down, new plants developing. Sections deliberately planted in upright position seldom grow.

CORINNE, UTAH

Divorce lawyers were not as greedy in the 80's as they are today. You could even get unhitched by slot machine. The ad in the Corinne UTAH REPORT-ER said so. "Divorces Secured — Presence Unnecessary — Fee $2.50".

Above the legal firm name of Johnson and Underdunk was the message that any disenchanted mate was invited to use the elaborate and complicated machine in the offices of the firm. The suing party simply inserted a $2.50 gold piece in the maw of the contraption, gave the crank a turn and presto, in hand was a beautifully prepared divorce decree signed by the Corinne City Judge. When the names of both parties were filled in the blank spaces the document was legal.

There was even more. In the event you were too busy to visit the office, you could simply mail the money and necessary names to Johnson and Underdunk. They would turn the crank themselves and mail the papers to you.

It was a grand idea for a while — and then the firm was in big trouble. It seems that as slot-machine divorcees tried to remarry, some found their divorces illegal and those who had married again found themselves living in bigamy. About 2,000 of such divorces were being threshed out in court at one time.

But before divorces, even before Corinne, Mark A. Gilmore and five companions stood on the west bank of the Bear River, looking out over a stretch of grassy, level land. It was in 1868 and inspired by

Joseph Smith's visions, Gilmore had some of his own. A thriving "gentile" city would rise here. It would become a throbbing railroad and steamboat center that would overshadow Brigham Young and his Mormon Empire. Even though Gilmore's partners were not endowed with such visions, they could work to create a great future for a city here, one that would have financial benefit for themselves. The group lost no time in securing the land cheaply.

The next step was to lay out a townsite with a business center surrounded by lots. Much dickering with the Union Pacific Railroad resulted in a contract to establish a railway station in the new city in return for railroad ownership of every other lot and free land for right of way and yards.

The Union Pacific saw advantages. East and west rail-laying crews were working and would meet at nearby Promontory next year, but that place was composed of salt flats at the edge of Great Salt Lake and would not do as a loading point for the stock and farm products expected to be produced. The new town, to be called Corinne, was on the banks of the Bear River and so connected to deep water — the lake. Ore from the booming mines at the south end of the lake could also be counted on to swell freight revenues. Mark Gilmore and his cohorts were equally happy. To have the powerful railroad behind them would be a big help in the days ahead when all this progress collided with Brigham Young's resistance.

Within two weeks of founding, Corinne was a town in fact with more than 300 frame shacks and tents, and more being built to accommodate a boom population of 1500, not including the 5,000 Chinese laborers employed by the railroad. The town had been founded on the premise that it would be strictly "gentile", meaning "no Mormons allowed". The field was wide open for any sort of boomer, hustler, gambler, prostitute or any other drifter as long as he or she was not of the Mormon faith. All this created a situation outside the law. When the east-west rail connections were made in 1869, the wild atmosphere was intensified by thousands of "freighters" who swarmed into the "Burg on the Bear", most of them rough, tough adventurers fresh from the Civil War and steamed up with elemental desires.

Corinne was shortly able to accommodate them in all ways. During its most flamboyant period it boasted of 19 saloons, 2 dance halls, 2 theaters, one of which had "the gaudiest stage in Utah," innumerable gambling dens and 80 women sometimes referred to as "soiled doves". With all this going on, Corinne was a thorn in the flesh of Brigham Young. He issued an edict forbidding any of his faithful to go near the place, which may have challenged some stalwart Mormons to visit the seat of iniquity if for no other reason than to satisfy their curiosity.

Early development included smelters to process the rich gold and silver ores shipped in from mines to the south. Residue, such as slag and tailings, were used to pave the streets. Recovery of the precious metals seldom equaled assay values, a fact to be expected in the days of primitive milling and smelting methods. As processes improved, someone thought of the slag-paved streets, assayed some samples and found them still worth working. So back to mud went the streets and into the mills went the paving materials, which resulted in some gold being recovered. It could be said — "Corinne's streets were literally paved with gold." Everything considered, the mills and smelters proved successful, about the only promotion effort that was with the exception of the exploitation of sin. Almost every effort to "improve our fair city" failed dismally. Brigham Young was behind many of the failures and natural forces spiked the others. The "Burg on the Bear" fought desperately to make itself the junction of the Union Pacific and Central Pacific but the Mormon leader easily influenced the lines to meet at Ogden instead. The "Gentile City" became the butt of crude and sarcastic jokes as business interests departed for Ogden.

Then there was the grandiose plan, far beyond the financial capacities of the town, to found an agricultural empire by creating a huge irrigation system using Bear River water. The promoters petitioned Congress for aid and a grant of public lands for the purpose with the argument: "It is the only

JOINING OF RAILS EAST AND WEST was fulfillment of American dream of spanning continent. On May 10, 1869, Central Pacific's Jupiter rolled over last-laid rails to meet Union Pacific's No. 119. This photo of memorable occasion hangs on wall of Corinne's old depot, now rail museum.

LONELY REMNANTS of Corinne's earliest days are livery stable at right, first bank at left. Front half of latter is of frame construction, rear of brick comprising almost impregnable unit centered by even more solid brick vault. Later growth of town demanded larger bank and increased jail facilities. When new bank was completed, old one was converted to hoosegow, vault serving as security confinement.

place where a purely American community can be brought into permanent and successful contact with the Mormon population whose feet have trodden and who hold in their relentless grasp every other Valley in Utah. . . It is a notorious fact that everywhere in this territory the Mormon Prophet and his coadjutors have acquired control of the water courses issuing from the mountain sides that can be used for irrigation, and of all the canyons that afford any valuable timber within reach of cultivated lands. This monopoly . . . has enabled them to confine immigration to those of their own creed." A bill giving effect to this petition was introduced to the House and Senate but nothing came of it.

Next, in 1871, the town tried its hand at steamboating. The 70-foot, three-decker *City of Corinne* was built and proudly launched that year. It steamed down the Bear and into Salt Lake with a cargo of machinery consigned to Lake Point, returning with a load of ore from the mines in the Tintic and Oquirrh Mountains. The venture was hailed as a huge success but the city fathers had failed to take into account the fluctuating level of the inland sea. The lake had attained a high after the boat launching and from then on dropped steadily until over 480 square miles of land were uncovered, the water becoming so low the majestic steamer was mired on the bottom time and again. Renamed the *General Garfield*, it became an excursion boat only to fail as that and come to an end as a pavillion at Garfield Beach.

The NEW YORK WORLD in 1870 had this item: "Corinne proposes to remove the capitol of Utah from Salt Lake City to Corinne, which containing but a few Mormons, is deemed a fitter place to put the military corps in." Obviously, from this account, some Mormons had crept in Corinne but the effort came to naught.

Possibly the best known Mormon hater in the territory and one who was not afraid to say so, was General Patrick Connor, the soldier-prospector who had helped found gold, copper and silver towns to the south. Connor headed the Liberal political party which had its stronghold in Corinne. A convention held there in 1870 nominated General George E. Maxwell for Congress. Campaigning speakers and newspaper stories made a point of condemning polygamy, this alienating not only Mormons but the so-called "Godbeites", who although having left the Mormon Church, still retained what they felt were the best features including plural marriage. Maxwell was roundly defeated although as the NEW YORK HERALD caustically commented: "The gentile town of Corinne polled more votes than it had inhabitants", many such votes were cast by registered but transient railroad workers. Maxwell ran again two years later playing down mention of polygamy but again was defeated.

1872 brought another blow to the hard-luck community in the form of a diphtheria epidemic which caused several hundred deaths and frightened many families away. A few years later Indians were attacking frequently and although the eventual arrival of troops from Fort Douglas drove the marauders away, another share of the population had gone too.

The remaining farmers were discouraged over the effects of irrigation that brought alkali salts to the surface of the soil and laid waste to orchards and fields. A final blow came in 1903 when the road through town was rerouted over the Lucien cut-off to bypass Corinne.

Though shrunken to a remnant, Corinne's tiny population today proudly chalks up a few accomplishments. The town added much to the commercial development of the state and aside from being the first to stand up and "sass" the powerful Mormon Church, it had the first gentile school and floated the first steamboats on Great Salt Lake.

OPEN AIR EXCURSION CAR was used only in summer, Utah's winters being much too chilly. Surrounding mountains retain some snow even in July, although many streams have sources there, most soon sink into salty flats. Exception is Bear River, it originates in north section of Uinta Mountains in Utah, cuts corner of Wyoming, re-enters Utah, again loops through Wyoming and even touches Idaho, finally empties into Great Salt Lake near Corinne.

OLD PASSENGER CARS stand idle in yards, are full of rail artifacts in jumbled confusion. Lantern burned kerosene, long outmoded by battery type.

FIREBOX AND BOILER of antique locomotive present complicated array of gadgets, all essential to safe and efficient operation. Split firebox doors were opened and closed by steam pressure released by foot pedal, valves in cylinder just above door hinges. Gauge above showed steam pressure, 210 pounds usually maintained when running. At right of gauge are valves controlling inflow of water to boiler. Lucky was left-handed fireman, since he sat on right side of cab and leaned out window for observation, often forced to grasp throttle (Johnson Bar, upper right) and pull or push it for speed control. Bar moved across notches in upper surface of supporting bracket, heavy knob at near end preventing bar being accidentally pulled off entirely which would open throttle wide.

RUSH TO THE KLONDIKE

Gold was discovered in the Canadian Yukon basin as early as 1872 without causing more than a ripple of excitement. Just enough color showed to keep alive the hopes of a few prospectors who continued to turn up a little gold as they stayed with their more dependable trap lines. By 1887 some of these part time gold seekers were having an occasional look at the gravels in the tributaries of the Yukon River, among them the Klondike.

There was good hunting in its valley and good fishing at the point where it empties into the Yukon and often a band of Indians would be camped there. Californian George W. Carmack frequented the area over a period of years. He had a Tagish Indian "wife" and a small lodge in the area which doubled as a trading post, from which he ranged to trap and keep an eye on the creek gravels.

In the summer of 1896, a Canadian sailor turned prospector, Bob Henderson, found some gold in one of the Klondike tributaries, decided to go down the Yukon for supplies so as to stay a while and work the gravels, to which he had not made a formal claim. On his way he encountered Carmack, the Indian girl and her two brothers, Tagish Jim and Tagish Charlie. At first the two white men got along well and as was the hospitable custom, Henderson invited the other to go up river and stake a claim or two next to his own. He was however opposed to the idea of fraternizing with the natives and soon went on his way to the satisfaction of Carmack who resented the smug attitude.

Yet Carmack, who had been fishing for salmon, could not get Henderson's gold off his mind and took his mate and her brothers to the area. He prospected longer than planned and when on Rabbit Creek not far from Henderson's camp, he ran out of supplies. Because of their near quarrel he would not ask the man for food and nearly starved before he shot a moose. This was on August 15. He was ahead of the natives so while waiting for them to catch up, he got out his pan and dipped into the Rabbit Creek gravel. Almost before the top water and sand had been sloshed off he saw the gleam of coarse gold. The next few pans showed good colors too. On August 17, Carmack staked his claim with his Indian brothers-in-law each taking "one above and one below."

By the end of November some 500 claims had been staked along the creek which now bore Carmack's name Bonanza, an incredible number considering the scarcity of people, immense distances between them and almost no communications. Many miners were finding nuggets of values from $25 to $200. Then it was found the gravel of Claim 21 above Discovery Claim yielding an average of $3 to the pan, or about $500 to the cubic yard.

The men were so eager to work their gravels that winter they tried many methods of thawing the solidly frozen gravel, an almost impossible task then. Fires were built, stones or water heated and applied. By spring some had excavated a considerable quantity of gravel which immediately froze in average -16 degrees. And continual darkness was a bad handicap, the sun not rising at all or barely skimming the horizon for a few hours until spring.

When temperatures at last rose above freezing and streams flowed, accumulated gravel was washed out. In many cases a short period of sluicing washed out $20,000 to $30,000 in gold. Occasional discoveries of rich pockets of nearly solid gold so strained nerves already taut from "cabin fever" that many miners came near the breaking point. Further frenzied work accumulated that first wealth shipped down the Yukon to the Bering Sea and south to coastal cities of Seattle, Portland, San Francisco and San Diego.

The inflammatory stories in the 1897 press, wildly extolling the richness of the gold fields of the Klondike, fired the imaginations and hunger for excitement of thousands of would-be adventurers. More than three years of deepest depression had gripped the country. Banks by the dozens had closed their doors and business was almost at a standstill. Jacob Selcher Coxey led an "army" of 500 men to Washington to agitate for a petition to Congress for a $500 million road building program to help end the doldrums, then only well started. When the vanguard arrived at the capitol Coxey was promptly arrested for "trespassing on the grass" and before he was released from jail his army had evaporated. The incident left Congress nervous and made a deep impression on the public, now thoroughly aware of the panic's effects. Now here was something to whet the appetite — a gold rush — the first headlong plunge into new frontiers since the Cariboo, Peace River and Rocky Mountain discoveries, and here was a new generation ready to be set on fire.

In the newspapers of Pacific Coast cities items about gold in the northland began to appear inconspicuously. The Portland OREGONIAN of Friday, July 16, 1897, carried this one: "A Vast Gold Pocket — Marvelous Riches Of The Klondike! Millions Taken Out In A Few Weeks. The Ground Is Said To Be Littered With Gold." The story reported that a party had arrived in San Francisco from the north on the *Excelsior,* their cabins filled with gold with a value estimated at $750,000. The gold had been mined in the Yukon, it was said, and some of the miners had spent several years there suffering the most serious hardships.

The following day most Pacific Coast newspapers carried front page bombshells. The OREGONIAN now came out strongly, thick, black letters spread across the page — "A TON OF SOLID GOLD". The steamer *Portland* had arrived at Seattle from Alaska with another $700,000 in gold. (By coincidence the *Humboldt* had entered San Diego Bay just previously with somewhat more than $700,000). The Seattle POST-INTELLIGENCER was even more blatant. It's headlines were red — and two inches high. "GOLD — GOLD — GOLD" they screamed across the top of the front page. "Gold in Seattle is weighed by the hundred pounds. The *Portland* is in here from the Klondike! — most of it taken out of the ground last winter in less than three months. Nuggets range from the size of a pea to a guinea hen egg and are picked by tenderfeet."

In the next few days newspapers all over the country were to tell essentially the same story, with individual embroidering. The first noticeable effect was that Seattle, and to a lesser degree other Pacific Coast cities, snapped out of depression to luxuriate in a hectic boom. Schwabacker Wharf and other landings were glutted with people trying to get transporation to Alaska on the S. S. *Tampico, Excelsior, Portland, Torpedo, Willamette, Topeka* or any other available ship. And many did become available, abandoning scheduled voyages with scanty passenger lists to load the argonauts to the gunwales. What matter that they packed excited gold seekers far beyond capacity and safety? After all, plenty less fortunate had to stand on the rafts towed behind. It was not until overloaded vessels, many of them just floating, were sunk by tidal currents and hidden rocks, that authorities took notice and acted.

And still the eager and hungry poured into Seattle to wait for transportation, streaming from all parts of the nation, selling every possession at sacrifices since few buyers had money. Gone were businesses, farms, orchards, all bridges burned behind the frantic adventurers. And not all who made it to Seattle got to Alaska. The waterfront town was a trap for the unwary. Many men, forced to wait for ships, with every cent handy, had it slipped away by harpies and con men. It was not unusual to find men dead in the streets in the mornings, beaten and rolled.

But thousands upon thousands did get away. Two years later an efficiently organized voyage would take miners to St. Michael on Norton Sound near where the Yukon empties into the Bering Sea. There they would board a steamer for Dawson City, if the Yukon River ice was gone. But in 1897 all were destined to get to the Klondike gold fields the hard way or die trying. They had tickets only to Skagway, Alaska.

SKAGWAY, ALASKA

If ever there was a "jumping off" place, Skagway took all the honors. The end of a hazardous sea voyage up the Inside Passage, the beginning of the devil knew what. It had all the confused excitement of a gold camp, all the panic and breathless anxiety, all the nervous expectancy, yet it was only a kind of shakedown stage in the journey to danger and adventure, the gateway to Dawson City and beyond.

Skagway lay at the extreme north tip of Lynn Canal, an inlet penetrating a maze of islands right up to the very foot of towering mountain peaks on Alaska's mainland. Strongly resembling a Norwegian fjord, the water way ended in an almost level delta of soil and gravel brought down the canyons by tumultuous streams.

The same geographic feature that provided space for a town to grow on made impossible any near approach for incoming ships. All steamers were forced to stay far outside, unloading passengers and freight on lighters, most of them at first little more than rafts. Huge piles of supplies bought in Seattle by Yukon-bound passengers were hastily dumped on the nearly flat beach to be searched out and claimed by their owners. Often before the bewildered gold seeker could locate his belongings a high tide carried them away. Replacing anything was next to impossible in Skagway and many a luckless stranger was stranded without passage money home.

If he did rescue his gear he had two choices of routes to the lakes on the other side of the mountains which were the headwaters of the mighty Yukon River, this the only inland way to the gold fields. There was White Pass, starting directly out of Skagway and Chilkoot Pass, beginning at Dyea, an old Indian settlement a few miles from Skagway. Until the gold rush began there had been only one white man at Dyea, Sam Heron, operating the Healy and Wilson Trading Post. Indians working in a fish cannery at nearby Chilkat spent their money at Heron's post and on rare occasions a white trapper or prospector would come through. A year after the rush began the village had changed to a city of tents and a few frame buildings. After the turn of the century, when the railroad chose the other pass for the right of way, Dyea's buildings rotted and collapsed under the heavy snows. Today there is hardly a trace of the town, said to have more wickedness to the square block than Skagway, something difficult to comprehend.

Skagway, at first spelled Skaguay, differed in some ways from an actual gold camp. Where it offered two kinds of a living, one hard working and

"SOAPY" SMITH (fourth from right) in Skagway with some of his cohorts about 1897.

"MA" PULLEN, one of best known and most loved women in Alaska. She met each incoming steamer with carriage drawn by best of her seven horses brought from her former ranch in Washington state.

morally upright, the other preying on the prosperity and lusts of the diligent, in Skagway there was no choice. Everybody was there for one purpose, to get out as quickly as possible. There was no "respectable" section and if there had been any street lights they would all have been red. The legitimate stores, hotels, offices were all but obscured by the brothels, saloons and vicious gambling halls. Parasite or host — which was which? Many times the knowledge came too late.

The probable reason for all the unrestrained depravity was Skagway's remoteness. Although in American territory the place had its birth without federal or territorial benefit or regulations of any sort. Then again a large part of Skagway's sudden population was made up of escapists and the worst kind of criminals looking for a place to operate. The innocent, confused and timid were their easy prey.

Many of the criminal predators were on their way somewhere just as their victims were. The boom camp of Dawson City was full of newly rich miners eager for a good time with wide-open gold

pokes. But both spider and fly came up against Canadian vigilance. At the top of the pass was the border and the harpies were stopped, the Royal Canadian Mounted Police not about to permit an invasion of known criminals into British Columbia or the slightly more distant Yukon Territory, part of Northwest Territory. Frustrated crooks and toughs of all sorts had no recourse but to return to Skagway and set up business.

Jefferson Randal Smith, a suave, cultured Southern gentleman, was reputedly the most notorious of such bad men. Nicknamed "Soapy" from a come-on game of selling bars of soap on street corners with the spiel that some were wrapped in dollar bills, Smith was fresh from the fading gold towns of Colorado.

He found Skagway his succulent oyster. More than a thousand lots were sold the first few months. Hotels, stores, restaurants were springing up, sold and resold at fantastic figures. The Skagway water was too cold to drink so sixty-seven saloons offered suitable substitutes.

ONCE FAMED all over Alaska, Pullen House now stands in decrepit solitude. This picture was taken from railroad track. Behind photographer was simple marble monument marking grave of Harriet Smith Pullen. Although time was late June, apple tree in full bloom shows lateness of northern season.

The bunco man bought one of them in the fall of 1897 and found work for the shills and confederates he had brought with him, an unholy lot of footpads, thugs, ruffians, harlots and card sharps. From the prospects already in town he expanded his gang to around three hundred members, each proficient in his particular field of chicanery. Contact men and bunco steerers met every boat, glad handed passengers, weeded out the well-heeled with practiced eye and steered them to Soapy's Saloon where a free drink was the starter. A good percentage of such tenderfeet soon found themselves out on the street with a cracked skull and stripped pockets. Smith himself was never in evidence when such things happened, remaining a power in the back room. He emerged however to pose as a public benefactor at public celebrations, making a great show of helping widows, orphans and the sick. These deeds masked his activities for a time but they became too flagrant to conceal.

His downfall came one day after a victim complained to authorities who were waiting for such a chance. A vigilante committee was organized to confront Smith and round up his formidable gang. The group met in the city hall but adjourned to larger space in a warehouse at the end of Sylvester

Dock. One of the leaders was Frank Reid who had left Minnesota for Oregon, serving through the Paiute Indian War and going to Alaska in 1897. He was a sharpshooter with his rifle and went armed at all times as did many in the rough and tumble town.

Smith had spies everywhere and one of them carried news of the meeting to him. Whatever qualities he lacked, one of them was not courage. He took his own gun and walked down the dock, confronting the men at the meeting. Reid told him he was under arrest. Smith brought up his gun just as Reid did, the two shots ringing out together. The mobster's career ended at that moment but Reid lived on for some time and both were buried at the little cemetery above town. A stone placed on Reid's grave was inscribed: "Frank Reid, died July 20, 1898. He gave his life for Skagway." The other grave was marked: "Jefferson R. Smith. Died July 8—aged 38 years." Most of the Smith gang leaders were rounded up and jailed, the unimportant riffraff gradually disappearing and Skagway was a little safer.

Even before the exit of Soapy Smith, church services were held in the town, the first in a tent.

"Ma Pullen." Purportedly a widow, a long-time woman friend in Skagway said: "Harriet always says she's a widow but she had a lot of trouble with her husband in Washington where they had a ranch and once she told me he had deserted her." Whatever the case, Mrs. Pullen was left with four small children and the ranch including seven horses. When she heard of the gold rush and the wonderful opportunities to make a fortune in the North Country, she left her children in the care of relatives, headed for Seattle, was lucky enough to get passage to Skagway and arrived there in the fall of 1897.

The raw frontier collection of tents had a job for everybody and Mrs. Pullen was hired to cook at three dollars a day. Before long she was making pies of dried apples in off hours at a dollar apiece. Then she was turning them out by the hundreds,

SECTION OF FRONT DOOR of old store was photographed as wreckers were tearing it down. Attracted by sounds of demolition, camera man hurried to scene of carnage, afraid he was too late to record gold rush remnants.

Before 1900 houses of worship for Presbyterian, Catholic and Methodist faiths were established. Even Y.M.C.A. and Salvation Army centers were organized. A skilled photographer, E. A. Hegg, native of Sweden, set up a studio in Dyea. Since the tiny building was built of lumber salvaged from a boat it was anything but light tight and Hegg solved the difficulty by raising a tent inside. Later he moved to the more solid Skagway, eventually taking the trail to the Yukon. He made pictures along the way, developing the plates under all sorts of conditions such as inside small river boats and drafty shacks with the weather far below zero. Hegg has left the best record of people and conditions along the route to the Klondike.

Skagway's most famous resident was a woman, Harriet Smith Pullen, more familiarly known as

LOCKED FRONT DOOR of Pullen House mutely tells own story. Moose antlers over door are common sight all through Alaska and Yukon country. Porch faces Harding monument marking spot where hearty president made speech after full meal complimenting Mrs. Pullen and Skagway.

accumulating enough money to send for her children who arrived about Christmas.

The tall, red-haired woman kept at her pie baking until she had enough funds to bring the horses to Skagway to run a pack train to the pass. She was at the beach when the steamer pulled into shallow water, watched cranes lift the animals over the side to drop them into the cold brine. As each swam ashore, Mrs. Pullen seized it by the bridle until she had all seven in tow.

With a stout freight wagon purchased out of her pie money, two strong horses hauled miners' supplies to the foot of the pass where they were transferred to the backs of the other horses. As soon as all were loaded, Mrs. Pullen took her position at the head of the train and led the string to the summit where the freight was turned over to the owner.

The building of the narrow gauge railroad over the pass at the turn of the century made the horse

UPSTAIRS HALL in Golden North Hotel dating from gold rush days retains atmosphere although hotel is still in operation. Rooms have some modern conveniences and fine meals are served.

FRAMED COLLECTION of Pulleniana is displayed at Golden North Hotel, once bitter rival of Pullen House. Room also contains Ma's bed and other furniture salvaged from her decaying hotel. Mrs. Pullen loved to display medals presented by visiting dignitaries, also to "dress up" in Indian costumes. Picture at lower left was taken on sun-porch of her many roomed hotel. Another shows her in elaborate garden in front.

freighting business obsolete. Ma Pullen then turned her energies in the logical direction, to her cooking abilities. She bought a house and converted it into a hotel. There is history behind the house.

In 1888 Captain William Moore, sixty-six years of age, and his son J. Bernard, settled at the eastern end of the tiny valley that would soon hold the town of Skagway and built a comfortable home for his family. Being the first permanent whites in the area they enjoyed peace—for a short time. Then the ravening hordes of gold seekers descended on them "like locusts," Moore said later. Over-running his property at the foot of the pass, they ruined his farm. All appeals to shadowy authority proved futile so Captain Moore made up his mind—"If you can't lick 'em, join 'em." He abandoned his place and took off for the Klondike.

The pioneer prospector did so well for himself he soon returned "outside" by dog sled. He took the trail in reverse. Traveling much of the way on the solidly frozen Yukon and the lakes at its head, then over the summit and down the pass to Skagway and his home. Beside his gold he carried with

him a large load of letters, among the first to reach a world avidly awaiting news from the interior. One message was an appeal from Captain Constantine of Dawson to the Minister of the Interior of Ottawa —"For God's sake get more police reinforcements to us." Finished with farming, Moore sold the land to several individuals, the home to Harriet Pullen.

The indomitable woman set about remodeling the building near the new railroad tracks. Pullen House signs faced both the tracks and "Broadway," two blocks away. Bath, wash basin and toilet were installed in every room. Some years later, when she expanded the hotel with an addition at the rear, two such facilities sufficed for each floor, rates being less.

By this time Ma Pullen was the best known character in Alaska, the size and quality of her meals famous beyond it. She used no paid advertising but word of mouth carried her renown. She knew what people wanted and what they would talk about. One feature was the rich cream from several Jersey cows. When guests were served large

SKAGWAY TODAY — Golden North Hotel shows peaked dome at right. Charming girl at desk wearing "gay nineties" dress, was asked name of mountain towering above. "It's named Mount Harding of course," she replied. "He was the only president to visit Alaska.

UNIQUE LODGE BUILDING of Arctic Brotherhood. Fraternity was organized in earliest days of gold rush. Membership was at first restricted to those who had been "inside" in first year of rush, later expanded to include anyone who had worked at Dawson City or related mine sites through complete winter or genuine "sourdoughs." Facade was decorated with pieces of driftwood picked up on Lynn Canal beach, waterway of Skagway.

dishes of wild raspberries from the mountains they would find at hand an enormous pan of milk and with a ladle would skim off as much thick cream as they wanted. This sort of thing got around.

Many famous people stopped at the Pullen House over the years, among them Robert W. Service, Jack London, and President Harding. A monument in the neglected garden marks the spot where Warren G. Harding addressed a crowd of citizens.

One of the many stories told of Harriet Pullen is about the small boys who caught trout in the little stream running through the grounds then sold them to Ma. She would pay for them by barter with a doughnut or piece of pie. When it came to settling real debts with cash however, she was not always so prompt to pay. Once she hired Skagway's

well known mason, "Charlie" Walker, to build a fine fireplace for the lodge. Charlie did a good job but well aware of her tendencies, left a board across the inside of the flue. When he asked for his money Ma said he would get it in due time. Anxious to show off the improvement, Ma held a celebration and lit the fireplace for the first time. A thick cloud of black smoke billowed out and the guests scattered. Next day Ma upbraided the builder but got a controlled answer. "Ma—when you pay for the fireplace job it will stop smoking." She paid Charlie and he pulled out the obstruction.

Harriet Pullen died a few days before her 87th birthday. She was buried just across the railroad tracks in a lonely grave with a simple white stone marker reading: "Harriet S. Pullen. August 13, 1860—August 9, 1947."

ONE TIME FIREHOUSE stands with gaping windows. Many such deserted buildings in Skagway are in imminent danger of collapse or are being wrecked. Low level of timberline on closely surrounding mountains is evident here, Skagway being at sea level. Short climb up slopes brings into view numerous glaciers and ice fields.

BENNETT, B.C.

How to get to the Klondike? The White Pass route from Skagway to Lake Bennett and down the mighty Yukon River was only one of several ways. At least six "trails" were available, most of them not fit for travel. If a man decided against gaining the headwaters of the Yukon, he could go up river, if the season was right and he could get passage, which the earliest rushers could not.

The Yukon River, after passing the site of Dawson City at the mouth of the Klondike, flows on into Alaska and thence to the Bering Sea via Norton Sound. This is north of the Aleutian Islands which separate all-year open waters from those closed by ice much of the year. In summer boats could slip through the Aleutians into Bering Sea, Norton Sound and the mouth of the Yukon via St. Michael which was usually free of ice by the middle of May. If the steamer was powerful enough to buck the seaward current she could proceed to Dawson City, a distance of about 1600 turbulent miles. Such a trip required at least three months from Seattle. This route was in use after the first year but could be used for only a few months, and by the time regular service — within seasonal limitations — was established the real rush was over.

Eastern Canadian newspapers advertised the "All Canadian" route overland from Edmonton and there was the Dalton Trail. Among the objections to these were their lengths. Without transportation a man could not bring his ton of supplies, which the Canadian authorities required for entry, let alone food and other immediate necessities.

There remained the two popular routes — Chilkoot Pass leading from Dyea and White Pass, beginning at Skagway. The Chilkoot began in a narrow gorge, rising steeply in 35 miles to a summit of 3,500 feet. White Pass took another ten miles to stretch more gently from Skagway to a ridge of 2,400 feet.

Here is a plateau dividing Alaska from Canadian British Columbia. After crossing the forbiddingly cold, windy area the plodding thousands again encountered small streams flowing north into myriad lakes forming the headwaters of the Yukon River, the largest of them Lake Lindeman and Lake Bennett. Most miners stopped at the latter to build their boats, others choosing to avoid the treacherous White Horse Rapids by traveling on foot to the end of the trail at Lake Laberge.

There were many ways to get up to either pass, some fantastically impractical. The simplest and surest was to climb on foot but this was a herculean job. A man could get himself up easily enough but he had to show a ton of supplies to the Canadian police at the boundary or be turned back as a potential indigent. This meant shouldering as much of the ton as possible, carrying the pack a mile or two, deposit it beside the trail while returning for a second load and then repeat the process until all supplies were produced for inspection at the summit.

CARCROSS was original home of Tagish Kate who with husband George Carmack made big strike. Suddenly wealthy, couple went to San Francisco to splurge in fancy living. Kate, left alone one day became lost but was found by blazes she notched in mahogany banisters. Deserted by Carmack, she returned to Carcross, lived in simple log cabin, wore cotton dresses, but retained necklace of gold nuggets from claim. She died in 1917. A brother, Tagish Charlie, also in on Carmack strike, was honored by government, being given Canadian citizenship and white man's privileges in saloons. With plenty of money he treated everyone and himself to point where he was spending whole time in jail, winding up broke in old Carcross home. Railroad bridge crosses lake at same point caribou did. While in cups one night, Charlie toppled from bridge drowning in cold lake waters.

OLD CHURCH, now in near ruin, is beautifully situated with view looking north down Lake Bennett. Picture was made in middle of June. About end of August snow will fall, lake freezing deeply for many months. Avalanches frequently roar down steep mountain sides, especially as spring approaches in May.

Naturally horses were in great demand but the few available were unsuited to the slippery, jagged ice, mud and mossy rocks. At some steep points where the trail rounded precipitous cliffs hundreds of animals were lost, falling to their deaths or mangled and abandoned. At one spot during the height of the rush the rocks at the bottom of the cliff were covered by dead and dying horses.

One fantastic scheme to ease transportation of gear was dreamed up by some high U.S. Government source. Helpful Uncle Sam sent agents to Norway for 500 reindeer and shipped them to New York at great cost. $10,000 more was paid to get them to Seattle where a chartered ship rushed them to Haines, near Skagway. It was another bureaucracy fumble. The reindeer could pull and pack men and supplies on level tundra but not on steep mountain passes — and there was no natural food

like lichens. In a few months most of them died of starvation, exhaustion and injuries. The fiasco would have created a national scandal had not the battleship *Maine* been blown up in Havana harbor and diverted public attention.

The Seattle Chamber of Commerce was flooded with letters from promoters, schemers and plain crackpots. One man said if the Chamber would help him financially he could quickly perfect his invention of an airplane that could fly forward, backward, straight up or down. Another man was building a covered "ice wagon" in which two men could sleep while two others pushed. But even without these idealistic contraptions many thousands did make it to the summit and on down to Lake Bennett.

This lake with its neighbor Lindeman at the head of the 2300 mile long Yukon offered a down-river route to Dawson City, 550 miles away, but how about a boat? Few knew a boat from a bicycle let alone how to build one especially when they had to start with standing trees. And even they were scarce having been cut so far from the shore hauling was a problem. A few skilled boat builders made so much money showing others the tricks, they stayed on and were delayed getting to pay dirt.

Before the rush there was not one man on the bleak, wind-swept, icy shores of Lake Bennett. In one year there were 10,000 stampeders at the head of the lake. It was easily the largest tent city in the world. In the midst of all the boat building Mike King arrived with sawmill parts which he assembled and cut lumber for $250 a thousand feet which went fast to those who had the money.

Although snow and ice remained at the summit until the end of June it began to melt at the lake by the middle of May, after which the lake ice grew mushy and opened up in spots. As soon as chunks were floating clear there was an exodus of a vast fleet — skiffs, scows, dories and what have you. In a few days they had floated into Yukon Territory.

At one point the lake narrowed so much that immense herds of caribou were able to swim across. Tagish Indians lived here and shot game, the village called Carcross by the whites. It was here Carmack had met the attractive Indian girl Kate who shared his later discovery of gold on Bonanza Creek.

After negotiating these narrows, boats proceeded down the long lake encountering little trouble unless they were too early and met ice floes. Many crudely built barges fell apart when squeezed between the bigger chunks. However those who did start early, if they survived the ice hazards, were spared some torment caused by swarms of mosquitoes. Few men had the forethought to bring netting and those who did lived day and night with it draped from their hats. Yet far greater hazards were ahead. First came the narrow gorge called Miles Canyon, followed almost immediately by the much feared stretch of foaming water aptly named White Horse Rapids.

With all these problems and dangers many enterprising men not interested in mining itself began working on plans to make money by expediting travel from the head of Lynn Canal to the summits of the passes. The first of these ventures was a short

LAKE BENNETT is complicated many-armed body of water, extending many miles north and south. Extreme southern, or upper end, is fed by stream system having roots immediately below crest of White Pass summit. These are headwaters of one of world's major rivers, the Yukon. Starting only 35 miles from Pacific, it travels over 2300 miles before emptying into Bering Sea, separated from Pacific proper by Aleutian Islands. Miners heading north from Skagway stopped at first available site at southern end of Lake Bennett where they built boats to travel rest of way to Dawson City, first leg being long stretch of lake. Since little current was available here, many added sails to crafts, usually abandoned after hitting rapid current of Yukon proper. In this old picture infant town of Bennett was still essentially all tents. Later many buildings were erected, including Miner's Church on summit of knoll, left center.

railroad from Dyea to the head of the steep-walled gorge back of the town, the starting point of the Chilkoot Pass route. Next was the building of a steam operated tramway. Incredibly, dismantled steamboats were transported by this means to the head of Lake Bennett and reassembled for service to the lower outlet.

But the whole picture was even more radically changed by the White Pass and Yukon Railroad, promoted in England when efforts failed in the

the most difficult and spectacular feats of railroading, right of way hacked out of vertical cliffs, across swamps, ice fields, deep canyons and house-sized boulders, in some places the grade being as much as four percent.

With no heavy construction equipment, all work was done by men, horses, shovels and black powder. In one instance an entire cliff, 120 feet high, 70 feet deep and 20 feet wide, was blasted completely away. All men and supplies had to be transported by boat from Seattle to Skagway, all communications carried the same way. As rails were laid down from Skagway, they carried material to the end of steel.

Much of the line was laid along the sides of steep slopes, workmen often plagued by thundering avalanches of snow which buried everything. At one spot near the bottom of a gorge an enormous rock, estimated at 100 tons, fell upon two men. The weight was impossible to lift or move and all that could be done for the men was to erect a cross on the boulder to mark their tomb.

Construction was proceeding simultaneously from the Whitehorse end and the rails met at Carcross, July 29, 1900. A gala celebration was scheduled, the last spike tapped in. Top-hatted dignitaries gathered to watch the invited guests, led by a senior army officer, drive the spike home, each taking a swing.

Aim was possibly affected by pre-ceremony quaffing. The first blow glanced off the steel, the next knocked the spike aslant. Wild cheers rose from the crowd which was well lubricated. After several more dainty or dubious blows, the spike "bloody but unbowed", the visitors adjourned to the nearest Carcross saloon and the trackmen took a new spike and did the job properly. The next month saw trains running and while the main rush was over, the line was busy with organized travel and freight transportation.

It operates a regular service today, carrying large freight tonnage over White Pass. Passengers express gasps as the little cars — the original ones — careen wildly over the narrow gauge tracks. The trip suggests a vastly extended roller coaster ride — possibly the most spectacularly scenic one in North America.

United States, the capital provided by Close Brothers of London. A Canadian railroad expert Michael J. Heney surveyed and planned the route with most of the work carried out by American engineers and contractors. The project was one of

117

WHITEHORSE, Y.T.

The modern city of Whitehorse is anything but a ghost town. It has a population of 8,000, most of the people in the entire Territory. It is the capitol of Yukon, having taken that honor from Dawson City which boasted of 30,000 people in gold rush days and has fine air fields, hotels, restaurants and all conveniences of a thriving city. Whitehorse began to boom at the turn of the century when the narrow gauge railroad was built over White Pass, from tidewater at Skagway to the interior terminus at Whitehorse, and kept on growing slowly until the Alaska Highway was built in the exigencies of the second World War when Alaska and Yukon were exposed to attack from nearby Siberia.

As a supply center in a remote gold rush region Whitehorse became a real boom town, with all the roistering aspects expected with a flood of single men. After this impact the town had a more normal growth as the main stop on the long Alaska Highway.

YUKON RIVER flows swiftly past old docks at Whitehorse. In busy days of water traffic steamers tied up here, unloaded or took on cargo for points below. Concrete platform, middle left, supported large crane. Across river is site of old Closeleigh, original town in area. Above this point entire flow of river is confined between rocky walls of Miles Canyon only 30 feet apart in some places, torrent of foaming water rushing through gorge. Yukon here flows north to enter last of series of long, narrow lakes—Lake La Barge—then heads for Alaska, eventually spreading out over 75 mile wide delta to enter Bering Sea. Total length is over 2,000 miles.

But prospering Whitehorse does not forget or neglect its historic single street along the waterfront. On the river side are such remnants as old loading wharves and hulks of steamboats they served. Scattered opposite are greying, false-fronted buildings remaining from the days when hordes of gold-hungry stampeders came swarming over the passes from Skagway and Dyea, then by boat down the twenty-five mile length of Lake Bennett into the upper end of shorter Lake Tagish.

At the foot of Tagish a post of Royal Canadian Mounted Police made a second check — the first having been made at the summit of the pass — to see that no one went on down the Yukon without the required amount of food. And this was something of a bottleneck, impatient prospectors chafing at the delay while police opened and checked bags of beans, rice, flour, sugar, ham, bacon, tea, coffee, condensed milk and dried fruit.

RELIC OF GOLD RUSH DAYS is tram car, built to run on wooden poles instead of rails. Two tram lines were built to by-pass treacherous Miles Canyon water. The Hepburn ran along the west bank of the river, the other built by originator of idea Norman Macauley, followed east side ending at Closeleigh, long vanished, across river from Whitehorse. Cleared lanes for tram lines are still visible along canyon, as are rotting remnants of pole rails.

The next hurdle was a rough stretch of water into Lake Marsh, in itself easy going but its outlet one of the most feared stretches on the entire waterway, Miles Canyon. Here the flow of water from all the lake basins were confined to a gorge whose vertical rock walls were only thirty feet apart in places, forming a torrent of white water sweeping at express train speed. Pressure caused a high ridge to form in the middle to which boats must cling or be crushed to kindling wood against the rocky walls. In some spots the channel was deep with spinning whirlpools and in others rocky shelves almost broke the surface, causing water to lunge forward in a series of cascades. Squaw Rapids was the first of these, then mile-long White Horse Rapids where the foamy, snowy crests resembled charging ranks of white stallions.

The story is told of one man's adventure in the canyon. He had made the arduous trip over the

NOVEL SITE chosen for nest building by eave swallows. Sometimes called cliff swallows, they prefer locations near water for greater supply of insects which are caught on wing. Birds are expert masons, building nests of mud in closely packed ranks, equipping each with entrance spout for greater privacy.

SLEIGH was in regular mail service many years, equipped with double set of runners to facilitate turning. Museum is one of original buildings remaining in old, ghostly section of Whitehorse. Dog sled on roof is not relic, merely stored for summer. Sleds are still much used in long, snowy winters and dog sled races are held in Whitehorse annually, attracting participants from entire northland.

pass, labored hard to build his boat, loaded it with all his supplies and in this welter of white danger with the end of his trip almost in sight, came crashing up against a projecting rock, losing everything but his life.

Half a mile downstream he struggled ashore and dried his clothes at a campfire. Gathering all the courage he could muster he set out on foot back to Skagway. The next season he had a new outfit in another boat but headed down the same canyon like a cork at the mercy of vicious water. And his boat struck the same rock. He made it to shore again but this time he would change the pattern. He pulled out a gun and shot himself.

At the end of this run men were only too glad to haul out on shore to catch their breath, rebuild or

repair their crafts. The rapids were a proving ground, exposing poor or too hasty construction at Lake Bennett — especially the sparing of nails, scarcest item of all. One man who had brought plenty of them had some left over but instead of selling them for a fancy price at the lake, cannily took them with him down river and sold them for even more at the end of White Horse Rapids. Leaks in many boats were due to hulls improperly caulked. This was usually done with rags soaked in spruce pitch but it was natural to skimp on this item as spruce became harder to find every week.

Some of the rushers chose to stay at this resting spot until they were sure boats and themselves could make the rest of the river. Some enterprising individual set up a saloon and the crude shack soon had the company of a whacked-together hotel and other structures until the collection bore the aspects of a frontier town, acquiring the name of Closeleigh. Though roughly primitive, Closeleigh was never violent during its short life as the Royal Canadian Mounted Police discouraged any incipient rough stuff.

Then came the building of the tram lines — two parallel lines running along the sides of Miles Canyon, eliminating the danger for those who could afford the ride. The one on the east bank terminated at Closeleigh, the other at a point across the river where a twin town began to grow. It was quickly seen a single town had all the advantages in this country of short supply, so the only building in Closeleigh worth moving was taken across the frozen Yukon to the west bank town. This was named Whitehorse and Closeleigh was relegated to history.

BUSY, REGULAR STEAMSHIP service was maintained from here to St. Michael on Norton Sound. Water traffic was possible only in short summer period, Yukon itself is frozen almost solid in long winter, as is Bering Sea north of Aleutians. This chain of islands is geographical divider of climate, shunting southward warmer Japanese current, keeping ocean free of ice along Alaska's Panhandle. Each autumn before freeze up Yukon steamers were pulled up on bank to keep hulls clear of crushing ice. When river traffic became unprofitable, partly because of completion of Alaska Highway, boats were not returned to river in spring. Most are rotting, one converted to museum.

CHAIN OF EVENTS leading to writing of **Cremation of Sam Magee** by Robert W. Service began with steamer **Olive May's** being stuck on mud flats at head of Lake Laberge. She was caught in fall freeze up, became enforced home for crew for winter. Nearby was cabin of old trapper seriously ill with scurvy. Dr. Sugden came from Tagish near Whitehorse but found the man dead. Unable to bury him in frozen ground, doctor borrowed firebox of **Olive May,** cremated remains, turned ashes over to police. Later Dr. Sugden, while living with Whitehorse bank clerk Service, related story to him and poem was written, Service borrowing name of Sam Magee from friend in nearby cabin. Real Magee lived until 1940, dying in Calgary. This cabin was part of original Whitehorse and has been preserved.

DAWSON CITY, Y.T.

Winters in Dawson City are and were cold, dark and long. Here in the sub-arctic Yukon Basin the sun describes an apparent circle around the horizon the year around. In summer the circle is above it, in winter below, always dipped a little downward in the north and upward in the south. About Christmas time at Dawson City the sun shows barely an edge above the southern horizon for a matter of minutes, then gaining in boldness it exposes a bit more surface for a few more minutes each day. In about two weeks the full orb shines for half an hour as it rolls along the horizon. Although seemingly cold, even this brief appearance raises temperatures several degrees.

During the sun's short visitation there is a gray half light. The remaining hours are dark but seldom "black" because the sun is just below the horizon and the stars, moon or crackling northern lights reflect their lustre from the snow. Precipitation being comparatively light in this inland basin, cloudy skies are infrequent. Snow depths are seldom over three feet although strong winds often produce deep drifts, exposing the hard-frozen ground elsewhere.

Temperatures in winter average -16 degrees. The actual range is from an extreme low of -81 to a high of near zero. During extreme cold spells when lights burn constantly the air is filled with minute ice crystals and clouds of steam rise from poorly insulated roofs. There will often be a week or two in mid-winter when the mercury runs between the -50s and -40s and there will be mild spells when it rises to zero or even above for a while. This long period of freezing causes the ground to become so hard that even in mid-summer it thaws not more than a foot on south-facing slopes, causing the condition known as "perma-frost."

Those stampeders arriving safely at Dawson City in the fall of 1897 in the face of this kind of winter were lucky in several respects. They were early enough to find good claims along the creeks, although the best had already been taken, and most of them found space to live on, no matter how limited. When all available ground for quarters was gone at Dawson, the men quickly began to "squat" at the newer settlement on the other side of the Klondike River where it entered the Yukon. Housing was a serious problem with no lumber available except the little shipped in by boat between the ice breakup in late May and the freezeup in October or earlier.

Most men who had come over the passes and down the river in boats they had built at one of the upper lakes, planned to return to the outside by steamboat downriver to St. Michael. So now they proceeded to tear apart the boats they had labored desperately to throw together. The lumber went into houses or flimsy shelters depending on how skilled

DAWSON CITY IN EARLY DAYS— Low, rounded hill in background is "dome" typical of region. Light patch is scar of earth slide in distant past, called Moose Slide because of shape, small stream on far slope bearing same name. Indian legend says slide obliterated flourishing village.

DAWSON CITY TODAY—This was main street, Third Avenue. Modern school, post office, museum are several blocks to right. Town was built on delta of Klondike River, ground swampy in summer, roads and wooden sidewalks elevated above mud. Soft earth extends only about a foot down, icy earth below even in summer—called perma-frost. Sun, in nearly horizontal orbit (in appearance) goes behind dome at back of town, produces light "dusk" at midnight when printed matter can easily be read. Situation produced long day of picture taking for photographer, with frequent interruptions by clouds or drizzle. Temperatures were in 40 to 65 range, in contrast to those of winter when mercury drops to 75 below zero.

or ingenious the builders were. The simplest ones were those put up by men who had hitch-hiked and had nothing to build anything with. They made walls of rough, unhewn logs, chinked them with moss and mud and smoothed off the ground a little for floors. Roofs were of aspen boughs plastered with mud and windows, if any, a row of bottles set in mud. Other shacks were respectable enough, made of ship lumber, usually ten to twelve feet.

Under all the talk and activity of putting up shelter, the new miners became aware of uneasiness among "old timers" who had arrived a few months earlier. The fact uncovered was — the two supply ships due in early autumn had not arrived and the gold-hungry population now faced the very real specter of belly hunger. A few had brought garden

seeds and planted radishes and lettuce on warm earthen roofs in the spring but this fall almost everyone watched the pancake ice coming down the Yukon with great misgivings. The chunks would soon begin freezing together and thickening and that would be the end of travel for the season. Dawson City would be isolated from the outside world until the breakup.

Late in October the superintendent of the Northern Commercial Company held an emergency meeting in front of the Dominion Saloon, and the men heard their worst fears confirmed — the *Porteus B. Weir* and her sister ship *Bella*, due in August, had been held up by low water and more than likely would be frozen in downriver. All men without sufficient food for the winter were advised to hurry

CONFLUENCE OF RIVERS shown in view taken from near summit of dome. Main stream is Yukon flowing from south in distance. Klondike enters at left, waters of different shade coloring Yukon for some distance. Point of level land in left middle distance at junction is site of Louse Town with its once notorious White Chapel red light section. Traffic across river was by boat, then foot bridge, then three-lane, steel railroad bridge. Yukon is not spanned in entire 2,300 mile length except near Whitehorse, some 500 miles above here. Ferry crosses it here in summer, traffic crosses on ice in winter. Dawson City shows blocks sharply delineated by elaborate system of board walks where wide cracks discourage spike heels, rare in town.

down to Fort Yukon which had enough supplies. Then a piercing whistle blast was heard. Everyone rushed to the river bank to cheer the arrival of the boats which had managed to get off the sand bar.

And everyone turned to and helped unload provisions so the two vessels could get back down to St. Michael safely. In two days they left with a full load of passengers who would not chance a Klondike winter. Those remaining could concentrate on digging for gold and squandering it in the bistros.

Enforcement of law and order was strict in Dawson City. Buttermilk was not the prevailing beverage and men did not play tiddlywinks in their spare time or remain celibate. They were all tough adventurers yet killings were few, robberies rare.

While the Royal Canadian Mounted Police recognized saloons, gambling houses and women were all necessary, they were kept under surveillance and any undue rowdyism was subdued right now.

It might have been different if the strike on Bonanza Creek had been the first magnet in the area but earlier was the rich discovery at Forty Mile Creek downstream from Dawson, just a few miles inside the Canadian-Alaskan border. On September 7, 1886, partners Franklin and Madison had struck it after the failure of many including Ed Schieffelin of earlier Tombstone fame. A boom developed at Forty Mile which was just beginning to fade when the Klondike hysteria broke out. A ready-made population complete with police force of twenty men moved up to the new location to be joined by an additional twenty. The really rough element never had a chance.

The police combined several red-light districts in one, total membership 400 girls, establishing a new addition to the thinly populated Klondike City across that river. It was also known as South Dawson and the two-block, double line of cribs as White Chapel. The little cabins were fronted by wooden walks, the street being an impassable morass in summer. In a few months the whole place became known derisively as Louse Town and the editor of the DAWSON NUGGET, with a flair for hyperbole, reported: "The residents of Louse Town have made a big thing of what used to be a nuisance. They are holding louse races and betting large sums on the outcome. One man claims to have developed a speedier strain and offers stud service."

All ordinary price standards for services and goods went by the board due to freighting difficulties and the scarcity of men not engaged in prospecting or mining. Although wages were high, food and supplies were sky-high compared to prices outside. Shovels and underwear, both of the long-handled variety, were $20. Flour cost $400 a barrel. Eggs were $1 apiece, the supply depending on the caprice of two hens. Five minutes in the tub of the bath house cost $1.50 with a change of water, less for that already used and still warm.

Ways of making money were plentiful, when ingenuity was used. One good-looking girl auctioned herself to the highest bidder, the money to be held in trust by the Alaska Commercial Company until breakup. For $5,000 the successful bidder enjoyed

VIEW FROM DOME in southeasterly direction shows spot where fabled Bonanza Creek flows into Klondike, percolating through dredge dumps from left to right. Original discovery of gold that sparked world into Klondike rush was made on Bonanza in middle distance. After miners got out all gold possible by hand methods in network of creeks, dredges came in and at one point on Hunker Creek are still operating on third going-over, each time finding gold in finer flakes.

OLD POST OFFICE was imposing with elaborate tower. Here it is reflected in window full of house plants treasured in long, cold, winters. Months with little sunshine make artificial light necessary for plants' survival. One hanging is **Campanula Iso-phylla** blooming freely here in twenty-four hour summer daylight.

the young lady's snug companionship all that cold winter.

Those severe winters profoundly affected the course of living and mining in Dawson City. No buildings could be placed on conventional foundations which would shift on ice. Pilings were driven and many proved to be permanent, persisting to the present day. Pilings for the old post office for instance are decaying yet holding up the long abandoned structure.

Early Dawson had no underground sewage system or any provision for sanitation except a few outhouses which required difficult pit digging in solid ice. Public latrines came later, scattered through town with tickets sold for their use. In a year or so authorities worked out a novel system. A gang of guarded convicts followed a dog sled with tank up and down the streets, stopping at each house and business address. On collecting days, if the owner was absent, he would leave the door unlocked. The men would enter, pick up the "slop jar", carry it out to be dumped and return it. When full the tank was hauled out and emptied on the frozen Yukon.

Prospecting along the creeks of the Yukon basin was done in summer and all mining, following the first discoveries, used methods which involved washing the gravel, allowing the heavier gold to settle out either in the simple pan or in sluices or rockers. In winter this kind of elementary recovery stopped abruptly. Since the ground thawed only a foot or so, not much freezing was required to establish perma-frost at the surface which stopped the flow of water and congealed gravel as hard as rock. It then became necessary to thaw a section, remove the softened material and pile it at one side where it was frozen in minutes. When the breakup of the rivers came in May, accumulated piles of gravel were run through sluices and values recovered.

This was the procedure as long as surface gold-bearing gravel was available, which with all the miners working it, was not long. Deeper penetration by sinking a shaft was then required, generally by an elaboration of the easier method. Gold was not evenly distributed, allowing simple removal of over-burden or pit mining. This was uneconomical because the desired metal was found in pockets or concentrations usually running horizontally on lay-ers of gravel laid down in flows of years before. So shafts had to be dug to reach them, every foot gained by thawing, summer or winter. A fire was built on the spot to be worked and after the smoke had cleared out, digging was resumed. Then the whole process was repeated time and again.

When the shaft reached bedrock below all old stream flows, streaks of gold-bearing gravel were followed horizontally either to their conclusion or the limits of the owner's claim — and sometimes beyond. Trouble followed if the infringement was discovered, usually settled by litigation. Sudden death, as in similar U.S. cases, was frowned upon by the Canadian authorities.

Thawing was greatly aided by the "steam point" brought into general use after the first year or two. Steam boilers were brought up on ships and placed at the top of the shafts. A hose carrying a head of steam led down to the working level, ending in a sort of nozzle with a small opening. A miner could direct a jet of live steam at any point, thawing the material in minutes. The released gravel was lifted out in buckets by means of a winch and piled as before. With the faster system the piles grew larger, often reaching a height of twenty-five feet or more by spring.

Breakup was the biggest event in the calendar, huge bets placed on the exact date and hour the river would open. During the winter several stakes were driven across the river in a straight line. About the second week of May excitement would mount as the time came closer, a man being kept on con-stant watch for the first shifting of the markers. When this happened everybody would knock off work to watch. In about an hour there would be a loud explosion, followed by several smaller ones, and a narrow crack of black water would become visible. Other cracks developed quickly until the river became a heaving, jumbled mass of house-sized blocks of ice, moving slowly at first, then pick-ing up speed. In about two weeks the river was clear but for another week or two the beach would be cluttered with bergs pushed ashore.

TERRITORIAL AUTHORITIES are making effort to revive Dawson as tourist attraction, largest accomplishment so far being restoration of old Palace Grand Theater where visitors attend plays during summer celebration—Gold Rush Festival. Another project, less pub-licized, is renovation of pioneer cemetery. This photo made in old Royal Canadian Mounted Police barracks shows weathered head-boards brought in for repainting. When board is removed from grave, legend is copied, placed in corked bottle and partly buried at location. Lush summer vegetation soon covers all other marks. Boards are painted snowy white, letters black. Still visible on boards in photo are letters Y.O.O.P.—Yukon Order of Pioneers.

With the breakup came spring and its long hours of daylight and by the middle of June those hours had extended over twenty-four and on the several nights around the 21st, the sun did not set at all. At Dawson City itself however, it passed almost horizontally behind a low peak, the Dome, directly back of and to the north of the city. From about eleven o'clock at night until two, a kind of dusk settled, affording a psuedo nighttime period.

The night of the 21st provided an annual excuse for picnics on the summit of the Dome to watch the midnight sun descend far enough to skim the Ogilvie Range to the north and on the stroke of twelve to be almost eclipsed for a moment behind the highest peak. Nights were warm but there would be big bonfires all over the level plateau.

This was the time of year nature relented, holding back the frosts, ice and snow to allow flowers to bloom by millions. Square miles of wild roses covered the tundra, punctuated here and there by groves of greening aspens and spruces. Every open glade between these stunted trees was filled with sheets of blue lupine and *mertensia*, locally called bluebells. Continuous hours of daylight allowed uninterrupted growth and quick maturity, forming seed before the early winter.

The same respite saw feverish activity in the mines. The very first trickles of water were used to run accumulated gravel through the sluices, the owner full of pent up anxiety to know if he was going to be rich or "skunked". After a few impatient trials, a semi-permanent set up allowed more water to enter the upper ends of the sluices. Streams high up were usually small and often shared by several claims, used and reused until the once-clear water was liquid mud by the time it reached the bottom. Gold was allowed to accumulate on the riffles, the small cross bars on the bottoms of the sluice boxes, and after a few days a clean up was made.

The annual spring clean up varied in value from nothing at all to those like the fabulous one of Alex McDonald, who in June 1899, after scraping out the crevices behind his riffles, found he had so much gold it took twenty-nine mules to pack it into town. Nuggets were often detected as the gravel was dug, if large enough, or exposed in washing. Now and then some lucky miner found a streak along bedrock where there was a gleaming deposit, more gold than gravel. Many claims were abandoned or sold as worthless, the next owner finding a fortune nearer bedrock. Several of these yielded more than a million dollars.

But the river bed gravels were finally exhausted and things slowed up. When some late arriving "cheechahkos", or newcomers, asked where they might find some gold, they were told with sneers to try "up there on the hill." They did and excitement started all over again. They had struck prehistoric gravels where the stream once flowed and there was as much gold there as in the more modern beds. During the big year of 1898 the Klondike and its tributaries yielded $10 million.

During the early boom almost all trade in Dawson was carried on with gold dust as the me-

128

dium of exchange at $17 per ounce. The supply of the glittering stuff was carried around in pokes, made of caribou or moose hide with draw strings or thongs. Most dust and nuggets, over and above that needed for immediate use, found its way to the bank to be melted and formed into bars. There was about 2% weight loss in the fluxing process where copper and iron were sloughed off. The pure bars were then assayed, since the "fineness" varied, the best being worth $20 per ounce, and the silver that most of them contained allowed for at 67 cents per ounce.

Bars were packed into heavy wooden boxes re-inforced with metal straps and shipped down the Yukon to Seattle. One such shipment, made from the Alaska Commercial Company's dock, June 9, 1901, weighed a ton and a half. The early and grossly exaggerated reports of boats carrying a "Ton of Gold" were then to become fact.

There were several small fires in Dawson's first year. In the frigid temperature most of the stoves were fired to a cherry red and kept that way with flimsy stove pipes sticking through wooden roofs. When the situation became extremely hazardous, police stepped in. They made a thorough examination of all premises, pointing out the worst fire dangers and giving occupants twenty-four hours to make alterations. It stopped most of the fires until a big one gutted the entire business section.

This did not start from some foreseeable condition. Above one saloon was a cubicle rented to "one of the girls" and among her many customers was one gentleman valued for more than his money. The girl heard rumors he was sharing his attentions with another but he denied the accusation. The argument waxed above the boiling point and the girl flung a lighted kerosene lamp at him. The bonfire turned into a holocaust of massive destruction and in the rebuilding, all prostitutes were banished to Louse Town. This may have accelerated the construction of a footbridge to replace the use of boats. Bitter complaints by the girls were soon heard. They claimed that during the summer period when daylight prevailed the clock around, their customers felt conspicuous parading across the bridge on errands with obvious purpose and reduced their visits which put a crimp in the "cribbage".

For a few years Dawson City enjoyed a boom never before seen. But the "little man", with his pan and pick, and the slightly better equipped one with shovels and sluice boxes, soon faded into history. The rich and easy diggings were becoming exhausted, and while there was still plenty of gold it was necessary to use larger and more mechanized equipment. "Big business" had come into the picture. Knocked down dredges were shipped up the Yukon, put together at Dawson and were soon operating on the rivers. One of these monsters with a small crew could replace hundreds of men working by hand and the glory of Dawson went with the miners. Not all the men went outside, for the "Golden Sands" of Nome's beaches were beckoning. The new boom town located near where Anvil

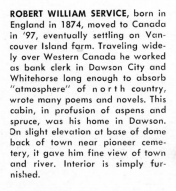

ROBERT WILLIAM SERVICE, born in England in 1874, moved to Canada in '97, eventually settling on Vancouver Island farm. Traveling widely over Western Canada he worked as bank clerk in Dawson City and Whitehorse long enough to absorb "atmosphere" of north country, wrote many poems and novels. This cabin, in profusion of aspens and spruce, was his home in Dawson. On slight elevation at base of dome back of town near pioneer cemetery, it gave him fine view of town and river. Interior is simply furnished.

GROUP OF GIRLS celebrate in front of crib in notorious White Chapel section of Louse Town, "suburb" of Dawson City. District was exiled from town proper when one girl flung kerosene lamp at customer in fit of temper, setting entire city aflame.

Creek drains into Bering Sea was soon populated with men drained from Dawson.

There were still occasional bursts of excitement over some new strike but the big frenzy was over. There had been a time when an ounce of dust was standard pay for a day's work but now it was six dollars in paper or cheechahko money. Many of those who had packed their outfits so painfully over the passes and floated them so dangerously down the Yukon to Dawson City would never make good now. Some who had brought a little money with them spent their time in the bars until it was gone. Others held auction sales, disposing of the belongings to those headed for Nome or some other strike, then left for home. And Dawson City settled down like a city come of age.

There were still enough people to keep the dance halls, saloons and gambling rooms going on the same twenty-four hour basis. The Palace Grand Theater where Alexander Pantages first made his name still offered programs with such stars as Marjorie Rambeau. Where a newspaper was a rarity to be read to assembled crowds by somebody standing on a bar, there were now several regular weeklies, the best known, the KLONDIKE NUGGET.

And there were still such characters as One Eyed Riley who won $17,000 in a single poker game. Going outside while he was ahead, he fell in with "friends" at Whitehorse on the way and lost $3,000

BELLE OF

PHOTO of classically draped female was displayed in every saloon in town. Subject seems to show effects of long winter diet of salt pork, beans and flapjacks.

in a game of stud. In Skagway he decided to indulge in another hand or two and lost the rest of his stake. The next morning he was headed back to the Klondike to recoup his losses.

There was always scurvy, sometimes approaching epidemic proportions, the waves following the lack of fruits and vegetables. The regulation "ton of provisions" brought in by one Englishman was composed largely of orange marmalade. He soon discovered the rare delicacy could be sold at outrageous prices and disposed of every tin for enough to buy a claim.

And there were still strange sights to be seen in Dawson City. One man brought a string of milk goats to Skagway to help pull his sled load up the pass and down to Lake Bennett. Many superfluous animals were butchered for food but the goats were pets and went on to Dawson City as the first such animals in the Yukon. In a town where only canned milk was available, the fresh supply from goats was worth a fortune. However when a friend brought in an orphaned moose calf, one of the goats was set to nursing it — with difficulties. The "child" towered over the foster mother and was unable to reach the source of supply. The problem was solved by standing the goat on a table.

Dan McDonald was one of the thousands who poured into Dawson City in the big rush period but instead of leaving after the bonanza days, he stayed on to make a home on the bank of the Yukon. He enjoys telling of the old days, particularly the building and operating of Dawson's railroad.

The maze of gold bearing creeks and their equally rich tributaries flowing north into the Klondike have their sources in a range of mountains to the southeast of the town. A pair of humps, characteristic of the region, are set on the summit of the ridge — King Dome and Queen Dome. The streams flowing on the far slopes run into the Stewart River and eventually the Yukon. They were also rich in gold, particularly the Dominion. In this area were concentrated thousands of mines, all clamoring for some easy way to get supplies in and gold out. A group of English financiers saw in the situation a

chance to reap some of the fabled Klondike gold. They formed a company which bought engines and track materials for a narrow gauge railway, shipping them to Seattle and Skagway, over the newly built White Pass and Yukon Railroad and at Whitehorse transferring them to boats which delivered them at Dawson City.

In the meantime one crew of local laborers, most of the men disappointed miners, were cutting ties from native trees and the Dominion Bridge and Construction Company started a three-span bridge to carry the tracks across the Klondike.

The first trip on the new line in 1906 was a gala affair. The train, named "Pow Wow", started at the station which was half a block upstream from the Bank of Commerce and ran to Hunker Summit, almost in the center of the teeming mining district. The main attraction here was a roadhouse operated by a Jakie Hartman, a favorite stopping place for those on their way to Sulphur, Goldbottom and Goldrun, small mining towns. The train passengers soothed throats made hoarse by cheering and several who wanted to make the return trip hanging to the outside of the engine had to be forcibly removed.

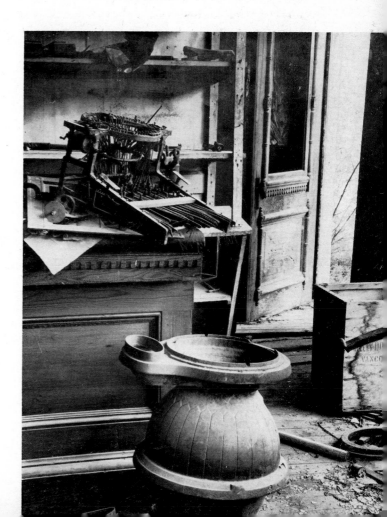

INTERIORS OF OLD BUILDINGS show great variety of objects. This curiosity on counter caused photographer many hours of research, leads resulting in no positive identification. Possible solution is in old Smithsonian photo of Beach typewriter of about 1860 in wooden case. Machine here could be "innards" of similar model. Keys were thrust into center to make contact with two-inch strip of paper running over spools at right and left.

LITTLE ENGINE, smaller than most, served as work horse in hauling dirt, gold bearing gravel, to localities more convenient for washing. It burned wood cut from nearby hills which was hauled behind in tender. Note "spike coupling" in front, requiring manual insertion of pin to connect extra engine or car to be pushed. At lower right behind bumper can be seen steam cylinders and piston drivers. Larger engines burned coal in plentiful supply from open pits at Carmack, some distance up Yukon, supply shipped down on river barges. Dawson City never had rail connection to outside world, line local only to serve mines.

After the festivities the railroad settled down to hauling gold and freight although a regular passenger service was maintained and an excursion run made each year to watch the midnight sun from the summit of King Solomon's Dome. One cargo consignment was a huge, knocked-down dredge for Goldrun. Gold was shipped in heavy strongboxes by the new Klondike Mines Railway Express. With all the labor and expense of building and maintaining the railroad it lasted only eight years when gold production dropped.

Dan McDonald, who had been connected with the railroad in one way and another since its inception, on such jobs as working for Guggenheim and

Co. loading trains with their derrick system, was on the last train in 1914. "Some of us had tears in our eyes," he recalls, "and some who were celebrating too hard actually bawled. It was really a sad affair and should have been carried off with some dignity. But a roaring argument got started among some of the boys and we almost had a knockdown fight on our hands at the finish."

The end of the railroad was a strong indication of the way things were going for Dawson City as well. It was never the same. Theaters, saloons and gay spots turned off their lights one by one and a fabulous era was finished.

PORT LUDLOW, WASHINGTON

"At Port Ludlow a man could be sure of $30 a month for a twelve hour day. He could have a roof over his head and hot meals. But he would have to work for them. The mill whistle split the foggy gray chill at twenty minutes past five. Twenty minutes later it blew again and the men sat down to a breakfast of boiled beef, potatoes, baked beans, hash, griddle cakes, biscuits and coffee. At six o'clock whistle saws were turning, logs and boards booming along the rolls in the wet, sawdust-filled air. And twelve hours later — every day — the men were paid spot cash at the company store." Thus does Ralph Andrews vividly describe a day at Port Ludlow in his HEROES OF THE WESTERN WOODS.

The first sawmill at Port Ludlow seems to have been that of red-headed Captain William Sayward and J. F. Thorndyke who had come out from Maine in the fall of 1853 and built a simple mill overlooking Admiralty Inlet. In June of the following year the schooner *Junius Pringle* arrived off Cape Flattery with Captain William Talbot and A. J. Pope who had organized the Puget Mill Company, and a Maine surveyor, Cyrus Walker, hired on a temporary basis. Pope remained on board. The other two explored the shorelines of the waterways to locate a suitable site for a sawmill, Talbot in the ship's longboat, Walker in an Indian dugout canoe.

They stopped at Captain Sayward's mill to exchange Maine pleasantries and marvel at the great expanse of fir forest, then found among the coves and inlets an ideal mill site at Port Gamble. But they did not forget the advantageous location Captain Sayward had.

By 1862 the big Pope and Talbot mill at Port Gamble was underway with a will. The partners were planning expansion when their manager, Captain J. P. Keller died. Cyrus Walker, still on the temporary basis, was offered the position on a permanent salary. He accepted only when offered the opportunity to buy a one-tenth interest. The operation grew rapidly with mills at Port Gamble and on Camano Island and in 1878 the company decided to build one at Port Ludlow. Captain Sayward's interests were purchased and a huge plant replaced the small one. It measured 65 by 394 feet and could turn out 100 thousand feet of lumber every day it operated.

With this mill well established Walker set about buying up immense amounts of standing timber, known as "stumpage", never more than a mile or two away from tidewater. The problem in logging was not in cutting the trees but in getting the logs to the sawmills. Much of the timber was acquired by taking advantage of the Timber and Stone Act,

REMAINS OF DOCK on which Cyrus Walker, Pope and Talbot's manager, welcomed visiting dignitaries who came on sailing vessels to the mill town. Much larger docks were located quarter of a mile to right adjoining giant sawmill, long since wrecked. Port Ludlow was situated on small deepwater bay on Admiralty Inlet, waterway providing access to Puget Sound and Hood Canal. In foreground lies twisty-grained log resembling stranded sea lion.

passed in 1876, which enabled any person declaring his intention of becoming a citizen to buy 160 acres of timberland at $2.50 an acre. The Pope and Talbot men, as well as other mill owners, made a practice of having sailors from their ships walk into the timber, then each making a legal purchase of 160 acres. They then sold it to the company at a nominal profit. It was a standing joke along the waterfront that the seamen never bought land very far

from their ships for fear of getting lost in the woods.

For several years Cyrus Walker had been paying court to Emily Foster Talbot, daughter of the captain. She finally accepted him and in 1885 they were married, the couple setting up housekeeping in the manager's house at Port Gamble. When the building caught fire and burned to the ground, Walker laid plans to build the fabulous mansion at Port Ludlow.

FOOTHILLS OF OLYMPIC RANGE (opposite page) look down on old log pond of Puget Mill at Port Ludlow. Trees are mainly Douglas fir making up "second growth" which has sprung from slash of early logging. Bound groups of piling, termed "dolphins" in marine parlance, remain from sawmilling days, floating logs shown being stored temporarily in today's "contract" logging.

The new home, called Admiralty Hall after the inlet it faced, was nearly a block long, built of the material so readily available, red cedar and fir. The bathrooms set the scale for all else — said to be "as big as kitchens". During the fifty years Walker was a power in the Puget Sound lumber industry three generations of Chinese cooks held forth over the enormous kitchen range at Admiralty Hall. There was a well-stocked wine cellar for the benefit of guests, Walker himself abstaining.

For most of the years Walker reigned at Admiralty Hall, Port Ludlow was the lumber capitol of the world. The position was attained after a shutdown, when lumber was being over-produced and causing prices to drop to unprofitable levels. Walker accepted a subsidy of nine hundred dollars a month to keep the mill closed and the company town had its first experience at being near a ghost during the several years when almost all employees moved to other mill towns. When prices rose, the mills again rolled and Port Ludlow gained a new and greater prestige. Its lumber and shingles were shipped to every corner of the world including South Africa where Cecil Rhodes was building a grape arbor.

Industry at Port Ludlow was not confined to sawmilling. A large shipyard was kept busy building such vessels as the three-masted schooner *Courser*, barkentine *Katherine Sudden* and the *Moses Turner*. Built for the Hawaiian trade were schooners *Waehue*, *Lihuluho* and *Luke*. Among steamers built were *Augusta* and *Hyack*.

Cyrus Walker and his associates cut trees from purchased stumpage as long as it lasted, then started cutting into their own extensive holdings, kept for years for the purpose. When at last that source of trees was exhausted, the mills were dismantled and many of the houses barged over to still operating Port Gamble. The colossal, soft wood mansion was turned into a hotel, at first elegant, then increasingly shoddy as time took its toll. Forced to close for lack of patronage it stood idle, transients "camping" in the once plush rooms. Then one night it caught fire and in hours little but ashes was left. Today the ghost town hunter searches in vain for any sign of the building itself. Still growing where the lawn used to be are old holly trees, maples and shrubs brought around the Horn to grace the grounds of a lumber baron's castle.

ENORMOUS MANSION built by lumber baron Cyrus Walker stood on slope immediately above docks and mill. Grounds were landscaped with shrubs and trees brought on ships from Maine, centered by brass cannon, veteran of War of 1812. It boomed on 4th of July and whenever company's ships sailed into Admiralty Inlet. Visitors welcomed into the huge center hall found walls paneled with native fire and cedar. House was filled with massive pieces of furniture also brought from New England. Highboards of carved bedsteads reached almost to ceiling, every bedroom having marble-topped dressers. Sideboard in main dining room was of walnut, hand-carved in Germany. Room and closet doors slid back and forth like those on ships. Widow's walk surmounting cupola afforded Walker unobstructed view of domain and access to flagpole of Sitka spruce. House was used as hotel in later years and became completely covered with ivy. After abandonment it burned to ground. (Photo courtesy Stewart Holbrook.)

PORT GAMBLE, WASHINGTON

When Captain Talbot and Cyrus Walker left the schooner *Junius Pringle* in June, 1853, in small boats, after sailing all the way from Maine, their object was to find a suitable site for a sawmill. It had to have its back set against many years' cut of timber and it must be flush to deep water instead of the mud flats prevailing along most of these inner shores. When they came to a small bay edged by an Indian village called Teekalet, "Brightness of the Noonday Sun", they knew they had found the place.

The oval-shaped harbor about two miles long had a narrow entrance to protect it against winter gales and many other advantages. Knowing the first white men here had been members of the Wilkes Expedition who had visited the waters in 1841, they named it Port Gamble in honor of Robert Gamble, naval officer and veteran of the War of 1812 in which he had been wounded.

Talbot and Walker recognized the value of the location immediately, and with the same dispatch returned to the *Pringle* which speedily sailed into the bay. Hardly had she dropped anchor when a crew of ten men was sent ashore with tools to construct cook and bunkhouses and other buildings, the lumber for which had been brought from California. The first native materials used were the cedar logs cut from the site to clear it, and squared for mill foundations. By a quirk, almost unbelieved by later sawmill men, the first lumber actually sold from the mill was white pine, brought from Maine by the *L. P. Foster* which arrived in September. There were 60,000 feet of the imported, "coals-to-Newcastle" lumber and the lot brought over $100 a thousand. This was the first profit made by Pope and Talbot in Washington, although their families were cutting trees and shipping lumber from their home area in East Machias, Maine, as early as 1767.

The *Foster* also carried to Port Gamble the machinery for the mill, which by that time was almost ready to be outfitted. It was 45 by 70 feet in size, built just above the high-tide mark. The boilers were fired and saws started turning not long after the *Foster* was unloaded and the first boards were "plowed back", being used to side up the mill until then open to all breezes.

The mill was not the first in the area. Mentioned in the Port Ludlow account is Captain William Sayward's little mill at that point. There was a sawmill at Fort Vancouver, owned by the Hudson's Bay Co.,

one run by Michael Simmons at Tumwater, Henry Yesler had one on the Seattle waterfront and there was a small operation at Port Madison on Apple Tree Cove owned by J. J. Felt. But these were all small businesses, the Pope and Talbot mill at Port Gamble being the real start of the Sawdust Saga in the Pacific Northwest.

Port Gamble's first little "muley" saw was able to cut about 2 thousand feet a day, that being eleven and a half hours. Logs were hauled into the mill by cable and drum, then hand-spiked onto the carriage to be pushed up against the up-and-down saw. In another year production had been increased six times by improved machinery. Four years later there was a new mill with modern twin circular rig having 56-inch saws which could cut logs up to 9 feet in diameter. It was soon producing ship spars and timbers 60 feet long.

LOST TO TIME and vandals is surname of young man buried in old cemetery at Port Gamble. Tombstone shows Indian name of town, Teekalet, was then in use, also that Washington was still territory, not achieving statehood until 1889. March of year 1863 when stone was erected did see reduction of area which previously included Idaho Territory, to present size.

It was dark inside the mill early in the day and toward evening, especially in winter. Illumination was by "teakettle lamps" which had spouts for wicks on both sides and burned dog fish oil bought from the local Clallam Indians. Results were a small amount of light, plenty of smoke and smell.

The monotony of long work days, broken only by Sundays, Christmas and Independence Day, was relieved by the "Indian War" in November of 1856. In the dusk of November 18, seven high-prowed, black war canoes entered Teekalet Bay. They were filled with Haida warriors from the Queen Charlotte Islands who made camp on the opposite shore, ostensibly preparing to attack the next morning. The sawmill crew hastily threw together an eight-sided fort of planks and at dawn waited inside for the expected raid. The 19th and 20th went by with nothing happening. In the late afternoon of the second day of "siege" the *U.S.S. Massachusetts* entered the bay. It sent a few shells into the Haida camp and the Indians departed as quickly as they had come. The next morning the sawmill workers were back on the job as usual.

Most of the white men came from Maine, a few of the crew being Indians. They were undependable workers, unused to discipline, with a habit of working only when the salmon were running, when they needed deer meat or when berry picking was good. Even with a steady job at the mill an Indian could be expected to take off for the woods or streams when he felt like it. Being expendable they were replaced when more Americans were available. Pay was $30 a month for eleven and a half hours, six days a week and the men got it weekly, in silver half dollars.

In 1858 the company announced it would "have the town surveyed and laid out into lots for the accommodation of all those who wish to make permanent residence here." In 1860, with a population of over 200, another notice was posted on the big bulletin board. The company planned "to erect buildings for all those who desire Public Worship, social enjoyment or fraternal communion".

1870 saw 326 people in the town. By now a hall had been built for dances and public meetings. In two more years Port Gamble ranked fourth among cities on the Sound and for the first time attracted a circus, in the summer of 1872. That same year the PUGET SOUND DISPATCH reported: "The town, which is owned almost entirely by the Mill Company, includes beside the mill and warehouses,

many neat and tasteful residences and presents quite an attractive appearance. There is the Masonic Hall and a school house. The only real estate in town owned outside the Mill Co. are the houses of A. S. Miller and John Condon and two large, well furnished and well kept hotels owned by John Collins, The Teekalet House is kept by Miller and Condon who minister to the necessities of the thirsty traveler."

By this time the school had about 40 pupils being taught by two teachers. The "exhorbitant" salaries paid the "principal" teacher, $90 a month, and his assistant, $50, were the cause of a bitter controversy. One resident wrote "There is much ire over this expenditure. It is thought by many that the school board faces bankruptcy, and that the school directors are trying to give their children a college education at the expense of the poor man's children who, because of lack of funds, will not be taught even to read and write. The large salaries are attracting many teachers to Port Gamble, there being 30 applicants in 1872 as against 2 in 1870."

Luella Buchanan in her History of Kitsap County, records that "February, 1874, a library was established through the agency of the preacher, school principal and Cyrus Walker and on Christmas of that year it received a gift of 200 books. Also the Amateur Theatrical Club gave a play which netted enough to buy an organ for the Hall."

That same year Port Gamble's steady growth faltered somewhat in a business depression when many men "left for the mines" but soon steadied and went ahead until by 1876 it was reported: "The Exchange Saloon and Lodging House has 25 rooms and the grist mill is now chopping 60 tons of grain a month, enough for use of the mill and logging camps. There is also a good barber shop. Though not the county seat, the Superintendent and Justice of the Peace live here. Traveling dramatic companies find this a good place for shows." 1879 saw Port Gamble hailed as the largest sawmill town in the county, a position it held until 1885 when all had to admit the place was "fading somewhat".

The mill still operates, although on a greatly reduced rate. The main company buildings still stand, much as they did at the peak of operations. They are well kept and painted a neat, "New England white", still retaining the appearance that justifies the reference to "Little Boston." The structure prominently labeled "Port Gamble Post Office" houses also the barber shop and library which opens only on Tuesdays.

ST. PAUL'S EPISCOPAL CHURCH in Port Gamble was built by mill owners as duplicate of Congregational edifice in home town of East Machias, Maine. All imported was original landscaping. In face of abundant verdure offered locally, New Englanders brought from Maine various trees such as eastern maples. Most of these, planted near church grew crowded, were replaced by others.

139

PORT BLAKELY, WASHINGTON

When the Port Blakely Mill was put into operation in 1863, the fir and cedar forests seemed to stretch endlessly behind it. But the saws chewed their way through the logs so fast it became obvious that the island on which the mill was located could not supply enough trees for very long. Then the mill men got Sol Simpson out of Nevada with a reputation for railroad building. He took over the Puget Sound and Grays Harbor line which had been built across the neck of the Olympic Peninsula from Grays Harbor on the ocean, cutting through "enough timber 'til kingdom come" as the saying went.

Simpson extended the line into Port Blakely and to several other mills that needed logs. The offi-cial name of the railroad was the G. S. Simpson and Co. but it was familiarly referred to as the Blakely Line and its rails were the first to be extended so far east in Washington.

Simpson did not confine his activities to railroad building, making many improvements in yarding logs, cutting time and cost in getting them from woods to mills, waterways or his rails. Ox teams had been the only method used for pulling the big logs along the greased skid roads but Simpson said horses would be better and proceeded to prove it over the opposition of the old timers. But his satisfaction was short lived as along came that revolutionary new contrivance, the Dolbeer donkey engine, that ousted both oxen and horses as log dragging power.

WHEN PORT BLAKELY WAS A PORT. Sailing ships jam the harbor in days when Washington lumber was number one cargo. The **K. V. Kruse, Malahat, Mowtor, Oregon Fir, Forest Friend, Conqueror** were a few of the old lumber carriers that tied up at the big Skinner and Eddy mill dock. The **Alice Cook** and **Commodore** were two of the sailing vessels built at Port Blakely.

HERE WERE DOCKS that fronted town of Port Blakely and its mill. Rotting stubs have replaced wharves once covering acres of tidelands. Gone also is imposing hotel which fronted on dock. Tide is shown here at low ebb but at flood, water line reaches nearly to trees at left. Town no longer exists, is replaced by scattered suburban cottages and permanent homes. On clear days view of city of Seattle is seen between headlands marking entrance to bay.

Of prime importance to every sawmill is the log pond. Its function is to corral the logs in live storage, to hold them until the selected logs are conveyed into the mill, kicked onto the carriage which moves forward to meet the saw. Port Blakely's narrow bay was usually so cluttered with sailing ships from all over the world there was no space for an undisturbed log pond. But the mill owners had their eyes on the extreme end of the bay which was a mucky flat of mud at low tide.

The problem was neatly solved by throwing a dam across the bay, trapping a quarter mile half-circle of water. Near the center of the earth-fill dam, gates were installed which would admit the flood tide from the outer bay, then close to prevent the filled pond from emptying. The log spur of "The

Blakely Line" was built alongside the pond so logs were dumped into it.

During the heyday the Port Blakely mill was said to be the largest in the world. It employed 1,200 men and cut 400,000 feet of lumber a day. A shipyard was built on the bay not far from the mill and constructed among other ships was the largest stern-wheeler in the Northwest, the *S.S. Julia*.

When the United States bought Alaska from Russia, it acquired a few bonus items, one being the gunboat *Politokofsky*. Offered at one of the country's first "surplus sales", the vessel was purchased by the Port Blakely Mill Co. Its guns were removed and the ship put into service as a cargo carrier to ply Puget Sound.

OLD BLACKSMITH SHOP built of bricks from local kiln. It was established early to construct first "permanent" buildings, all of which are now gone except this one. In cool, moist climate of Puget Sound, English ivy luxuriates, thriving like native plant as shown here.

Until '79 the importance of Port Blakely seemed to be ignored by some of its neighbors. Tacoma, for example, suddenly became aware of lost opportunities when its LEDGER spoke up in an editorial February 29, 1879: "Blakely is the smartest town of its population in these parts, and a little trade with it would help New Tacoma immensely. Olympia now furnishes the bulk of the beef that goes in there to supply ships, steamers and townspeople, a new trade, by the way, gained by that city at the expense of Seattle." Also of Tacoma, the item conceded three inches later.

The port reached its peak period during and shortly after the end of territorial days. By the beginning of the World War it was almost dead, picking up somewhat during that conflict, then again lying back never to recover except as a suburban area for ferry commuters to Seattle. All shipbuilding and sawmill structures are long gone. Rails have been taken up, short sections being used for gate posts. Except for the stubs of teredo-eaten pilings, remains of the old dam and a brush-concealed brick smithy, few signs of the once booming town remain.

The town was described in the late '70s as being long and narrow, confined at the rear by the steeply-rising hills, on the front by the bay filled with so many sailing vessels it sometimes had the appearance of a "woods of killed and bleached trees". While the townsite had been cleared of timber, stubborn stumps remained and wagons going down the one "street" had to meander around the obstacles.

Other than the post office, school and several saloons, the most imposing building in the village was the new hotel. It had two stories and was proudly claimed to be painted. The gay structure faced the bay, fronted by a roomy "porch" which was really a dock built on pilings over the edge of the bay and connected to the wharf where passenger ships tied up. Disembarking passengers were easily influenced to walk the few remaining steps to the hotel where they could promptly alleviate thirsts and sign the register.

RUINED FLOOD GATES once controlled ebb and flow of tides to create stable log pond of small bay at right. With gate gone, all water flows out on extreme low tides, final dregs seen here spilling into outer part of bay. Dam has nearly disappeared, was built along lines of pilings seen in background, constructed mostly of soil, mixed with bricks from early kiln. Walls of gates are of cut stone, iron gates long since vanished, perhaps salvaged for metal during first world war, by which time Port Blakely was nearly defunct as town.

UNION, WASHINGTON

Lumbering has been of prime importance in the Puget Sound country of Washington since 1788 when Captain John Meares left it with his sailing vessel loaded with spars for China. The load never reached there, the ship running into a heavy storm and the cargo jettisoned. Several years later when Captain George Vancouver's ship lost a spar, he had his men cut a tree in the Washington woods to replace it. Then fur trading became well established and the need for log cabins created a new industry. Millwright William Cannon set up a whipsaw platform at Fort Vancouver in 1825. He sawed boards with this crude hand-device for a year, replacing it with a sawmill built with machinery from London.

The Fort Vancouver mill operated until about 1847 when the machinery was sold to Colonel Michael T. Simmons who set it up at Tumwater, bringing sawmilling close to Puget Sound. In 1852 residents of the Alki Point settlement, later to be part of Seattle, cut trees on the hills back of the village for use as pilings. They brought oxen from the Puyallup Valley to haul the logs to the water, this probably being the first operation of its kind. A sawmill owned by Nicjolas De Lin in Tacoma sawed 2,000 feet a day. De Lin's boards sold only while there was no competition for his saws invariably cut them "on the bias", tapered from end to end or in both directions from the middle.

Henry Yesler's first steam sawmill in 1853 at Seattle was the beginning of the big time in the lumber industry and mills now spread along Hood Canal, actually a natural inlet from the Strait of Juan de Fuca. The Olympia COLUMBIAN reported in 1853: "There are now no less than fourteen sawmills run by water power and one steam sawmill in process of construction on Puget Sound. A large number of our citizens are getting out cargoes of hewn timber, piles, shingles and cordwood faster than the number of vessels engaged in that trade can carry them to market."

The shores of Hood Canal were becoming dotted with logging camps and small sawmills, with no central source of supplies. In 1858 partners Wilson and Anderson set up a trading post on the south shore of the Canal at the narrow neck of land con-

necting the Kitsap Peninsula to the Olympic Peninsula and the mainland. This strategic situation commanded a view of Hood Canal and ships in both northeasterly and northwesterly directions, the Canal making a right angle bend at that point.

As soon as the trading post was well established, the Rush House was built. It was a grand affair, two stories high with six bedrooms (guests supplying their own bedding) and most important, a bar where all sorts of potables could be had. The dining room served "elegantly complete" meals. To make sure no guests were absent when dinner was served, the cook went out on the balcony and sent out a couple of blasts from a cow's horn fitted with a shrill-sounding reed.

After a few years Anderson tired of keeping up his end of the trading post work and sold his share to F. C. Purdy. In a few more years the enterprise was transferred to the ownership of John McReavy, until then a lumberman. By 1876 there were at least fifty logging camps in the area, most of them buying all their provisions at the trading post. By 1889 the land around the store and hotel was becoming so well settled it was platted as a town and christened Union City. Growth had been slow but steady yet Union City was to regret things could not stay that way.

Around 1890 rumors were rife that Union City would be at the crossroads of several railroads — the Grays Harbor and Puget Sound, the Union City and Naval Station, and Port Townsend and Southern Lines. As a consequence Union City boomed so fast lots that had been worth next to nothing now sold for $1,000 each. So many people moved into the town there was no place for them to live, in spite of earnest efforts of the one sawmill, brand new, to turn out enough lumber for new houses. Tents blossomed everywhere, even along the beach. More than one greenhorn from the midwest pitched his tent when the tide was out, only to find his domicile flooded a few hours later. Meals were cooked over communal fires until stoves could be obtained.

Further inflation came with the arrival of construction crews, horses and Union Pacific equipment. On the very day work was to start came devastating news. Baring Brothers Bank of London refused further payments on its outstanding debts

HOME OF JOHN McREAVY who bought and operated town's early day trading post, platted and named Union City in 1889. Sawmill built by McReavy cut cedar boards lining interior walls of house. Building, erected in 1889, was once painted bright yellow, is now mellowed by age. It has ground level basement at rear where hand laundry was once operated by Indian women. House is now home of Mr. and Mrs. Lud Anderson. Mrs. Anderson was Helen McReavy, daughter of John, has written history—**How, When and Where on Hood Canal.**

of twenty-one million pounds, obligations assumed in a fantastic web of international finance. The panic of 1893 was on and all railroad work was immediately canceled. Union City's dream of becoming a rail terminus at salt water skittered away, the boom at an end. In embarrassment the town quickly dropped the "City" from its name and as plain Un-

ion, settled back to the simple existence it has since led. In recent years, with rapid transportation available, summer residents have built cottages along the shores of Hood Canal. Restaurants, stores and other small businesses have sprung up at Union, causing small scale prosperity, likely to prove more permanent than the first.

dent of Toronto University) taught school and with the proceeds we lived while the other two built houses and cleared land for the gardens. After the short space of 16 months we were practically out of debt. Incoming members aided us with payments for land and membership fees. Today we have 22 members, 14 adult male workers, have 11 houses erected and another cost $300 well under way; bought and paid for two teams of horses, but sold one recently. This success is the result of our labors as none of the incoming members had means to aid them."

Allen went on working hard said the item of January 1, 1899: "Comrade Allen has his hands full these days teaching singing classes, writing copy for advertising in DISCONTENT, all voluntary and without pay. Yet, there are those who say that in Anarchy where money is eliminated there would be no incentive to labor." In another issue was this bit: "Comrade C. W. Fox has rheumatism. He says it is nobody's business, though, that he can be sick if he wishes." And every issue carried this note: "How to get here. Parties inclining to visit us will come to Tacoma and take steamer *Tycoon* for Joe's Bay, leaving Commercial Dock every day except Saturday and Sunday at 2:30. Ask Captain to let you off on Joe's Bay raft." Presumably, someone in the colony would row out and bring the visitor ashore.

By 1900 Home's population was seventy-five, including thirty school children. DISCONTENT had claimed a circulation of twelve hundred, it being obvious the paper was intended for outside propaganda. One of these readers was Emma Goldman, feminist radical, who wrote essays for the publication on free love in which she invariably blamed the organized church for prostitution.

Although Home was getting a reputation for being a retreat for those who advocated free love, sin and anarchy, there was no serious focus of attention on the doings there until the assassination of President McKinley in 1904. Home could not be suspected of harboring the actual assassin, Leon Czolgosz, but it was a known refuge for anarchists like him. In the hysteria following the President's death, a group calling itself Loyalty League held a mass meeting in Custer Hall in Tacoma. Members formed a Vigilante Committee whose express purpose was to go to Home and "subdue" the colonists. The Tacoma LEDGER reported that the Committee should charter a steamer, go to Home, run off the members and burn their town.

While the excited Committee members were discussing ways and means, the pastor of the German

Evangelical Church of Tacoma, Rev. J. F. Doescher, made a trip to the colony, interviewed members in their houses and preached a sermon in their Liberty Hall. When he returned to Tacoma he went straight to the LEDGER office and demanded that the paper see to it that any raid on the colonists be prevented. "They have made clearings", he said, "planted orchards, made gardens. The people are sober, industrious and friendly. Their neighbors give them good witness. They are better citizens by far than those that have been shouting 'Exterminate the vipers!' "

The newspaper did discourage the raid, possibly because destruction of the colony would ruin a good news source. But Home was not out of the woods. The postal authorities took over, sending the United States marshall over to arrest Goven and his helpers for "depositing obscene matter in the U.S. Mails."

As a gesture of passive non-resistance, Home members greeted the marshall at the gangplank, made him a guest of honor at a dinner and later at a dance. The marshall dined, danced and next morning escorted his prisoners to the Tacoma jail. The LEDGER had a large type heading next day to the effect that the intrepid law officer had single-handedly attacked, subdued and arrested the miscreants at great personal danger to himself. The DISCONTENT cried out at the injustice, attempted to have the LEDGER retract the statements and when it failed to do so, the newspaper was branded in the colony's own as "not being interested in simple truth."

The trial was held on March 11, 1902. Goven and his associates were acquitted but authorities held one more trump. In April the Home post office was removed by order of the Postmaster General. Shortly afterward the DISCONTENT was deprived of its mailing privileges and that finished the paper.

Following a new established pattern, another new publication was created from the old, THE DEMONSTRATOR, with Morton listed as publisher and Goven as printer. The appearance was familiar and so was the approach. It also reminded outsiders: "If you should consider coming to us to live you should consider several things. There is much hard work to be done. We have cleared rough streets but still lack sidewalks. While there are eleven cows here now, there still is not enough milk for our needs. Most important consideration however, is that you will be able to live under the anarchist plan, that you may do just as you please as long as you do not infringe upon the natural rights of others."

Indicating some satisfaction in the way things were proceeding, was this item: "How does a com-

EARLY COTTAGES built by colonists stood in open, old growth trees having been cut for wood. Lusty, brushy second growth has all but covered some houses falling into decay through abandonment. This house provided excellent view of harbor entrance, is not now visible except to searchers of relics of colony days.

munity of eighty people, with two newspapers, one weekly, one monthly, a school with two teachers, no saloons, no churches, no policemen and no jails compare with what you have been used to?"

But now transportation troubles beset the colony, the newspaper reporting: "The steamer *Tycoon* has been laid up for repairs and our sole communication with Tacoma has been by means of the Dadisman and Adams launches.". . . "Our path along the shore toward Tacoma is being extended and improved and it is beginning to take on some of the aspects of a real road."

Morton did very well with THE DEMONSTRATOR for a time, as long as he paid strict attention to business. He was susceptible to outside interests, such as helping promote his friend, Henry George,

for mayor of New York. While in that city Morton neglected his newspaper and it died like the others.

What bothered Home the most or what gave the Tacoma LEDGER the most ammunition to fire at Home was nude bathing. The reports that the colony's beaches were filled with assorted human forms cavorting gaily in the altogether caused more than raised eybrows. Hundreds of LEDGER readers visited the place "just to make sure the truth or falsity of the reports."

What started most of the rumors was Henry Dadisman's purchase of two hundred acres adjoining Home. He opened the land to settlers, the first of whom were a number of Dukhobors from Russia. Members of the sect were accustomed to being undressed at home and naturally the same when bathing. Home colonists who had enjoyed such bathing privileges but had been discreet or in semi-seclusion, were now emboldened to the same openness. But there was a complication. A small neighbor village named Lake Bay did not share in these liberal views. Residents there protested that four people, two men and two women, were bathing in the nude across the bay. Arrested for indecent exposure, the quartet was brought before Justice Tom Larkin in Lake Bay court. One witness was asked how she could be sure the bathers across the bay, nearly half a mile from her home, were nude. She replied: "I have a good pair of binoculars and I know how to use them." Worst of all, it turned out the complaining witness was a resident of Home.

By this time there was a new newspaper in the colony, the AGITATOR, run by Jay Fox and it was he who wrote the editorial mentioned earlier—"The Nudes and the Prudes". The Tacoma LEDGER made much of the editorial and drew attention to the various "atrocities" committed in Home in recent years, implying that Home was capable of allowing anything. In the winter of 1910-11 the plant of the Los Angeles TIMES was bombed by anarchists, Home was immediately suspected of harboring the guilty men. William J. Burns, head of his detective agency visited the colony under the guise of a book salesman. The evidence he picked up there led to further investigation and eventual arrest of two of the men involved in the bombing. One, Matthew Schmidt, had actually lived in Home at one time. The other was David Caplan, apprehended in New York on information given Burns by a boy named Donald Vose living in Home.

Burns later wrote a book enlarging on his experiences. The volume had a wide circulation and it did Home no good. It included such distorted paragraphs as "Home Colony is the nest of Anarchy in the United States. There are about 1200 of them living there without regard for a single decent thing in life. They exist in a state of free love and are notoriously unfaithful to the mates thus chosen, and are so crooked that even in this class of rogues there does not seem to be a single hint of honor."

A few months later Fox's editorial boomeranged. He was arrested for "tending to encourage or advo-cate disrespect for law or for a court of justice. The trial, held in Pierce County Courthouse, excited much comment in newspapers nationally. Every detail of life in Home Colony appeared lurid when reported in the LEDGER. Nothing was said of the industry, frugality and general peacefulness of the settlers.

Fox was convicted, the jury recommending leniency. He was sentenced to two months in the county jail and while serving the time, the State of Washington elected a new governor, Ernest Lister, who pardoned Fox unconditionally. The editor returned to Joe's Bay, but things were not the same. Unfavorable publicity had been too much for the colony. The Association was broken up and people began to move away.

Jay Fox and his wife remained with a number of other faithfuls. Fox died a few years ago but his wife still lives in the old home across the bay with an interest in painting. The colony area is again populated, sparsely enough, by summer residents and a few permanent homes. Home's post office was never reinstated under the same name but the area is served by another at the crossroads about half a mile away. It bears the name of the colony's old antagonist, Lake Bay. In retrospect, all things considered, there was no place like Home.

SOME COTTAGES closer to water front have been kept in repair, are occupied by summer residents. Apple trees, here in full bloom, attest agricultural proclivities of settlers. Venerable specimens are small remnants of orchard of seven hundred assorted fruit trees planted on this bench above Joe's Bay. Beach below was site of many stories told of residents in days when reputed nude bathing caused big furor in Tacoma press. One was about two young girls called to mother's knee. "You're getting to be big girls now and shouldn't go swimming without your bathing suit." Girls, later observed sun bathing on sand in nude, protested: "We **did** wear our suits while we were swimming."

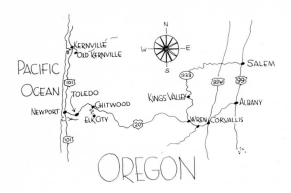

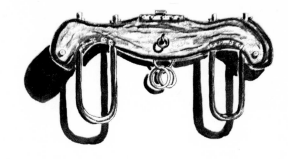

KINGS VALLEY, OREGON

The words had a deep and tragic significance. Samuel Parker, the wagon master, wrote them as they sounded. "We tuck what is called the Meek cut of", and later in view of what happened, he added: "A bad cut of fore all that tuck it." It was indeed a bad cutoff for all who took it.

Destiny interfered with the crunchingly slow progress of the wagon trains at Fort Boise. A number of them bound for Oregon's Willamette Valley met there, the emigrants exhausted and dispirited, yet trying feebly to answer the question — "Shall we keep on and if we do, do we go by the established Oregon Trail or follow this Steven Meek and pay him $5 a wagon? Maybe he's right and maybe he's wrong. All we know about him is he's a brother of Joe Meek who is a trusted mountain guide."

One party did follow Meek, the train of Nahum King, his young daughter Sarah and her husband Rowland Chambers. And then deep trouble began. The ox-drawn wagons were in the country named by French trappers "Malheur", meaning "evil hour", and so it proved. Sarah died, near the place the hamlet Beulah appeared forty years later, and a crudely lettered stone was set to mark the grave — "Mrs. S. Chambers   Sept. 3, 1845."

The procession toiled on at a maddeningly slow pace. In two days it stopped at a stream, a much disputed spot where, legend says, the children picked up gold nuggets and played with them in a little blue bucket which they hung under the wagon when it began moving. When the long journey ended its contents were discovered and the wild excitement caused many searches for the spot on the stream and many tales about the mythical Blue Bucket Mine, which was never found. The weary emigrants did not join in the hunt or lift their spirits in wondering. They were just thankful to be

YOUNG LT. GARBER just couldn't win, even at the end. Tombstone, paid for by collection among soldiers stationed at Fort Hoskins came from stone-cutters with "r" in name transposed to "s," was erected anyway.

GRIST MILL, built in summer of 1854, is among oldest in Oregon country. Located on banks of Luckiamute River, it utilized water power generated by overflow from rock dam built by partners Rowland Chambers and A. H. Reynolds. Upper story was storage space for grain to be ground.

able to settle down in the peaceful valley with no wish to return to the place of tribulation even if they found it.

The fertile little valley the Nahum King family and widowed Rowland Chambers selected was separated from the Willamette Valley by a low line of hills. It came to be called Kings Valley and the apostrophe, if any, has long since disappeared.

The lonely Chambers wooed and won another of King's daughters. He built a little house and planted a large acreage in wheat as did most early settlers there. But instead of shipping out his grain, he built a grist mill on the creek called Luckiamute. By means of a stone dam he was able to get enough fall in the slow moving creek to turn an old-fashioned water wheel which transferred power to the

mill higher on the bank by means of huge, hand-made leather belts. Chambers had an able partner in the project, A. H. Reynolds, whose lately discovered diary records the time of construction "We started work on the grist mill in June, 1854."

On April 13 of the next year the Kings Valley post office was established with Rowland Chambers as first postmaster. From then on the town grew rapidly, supporting a sawmill, store and several saloons. Although a log school house dated as early as 1849, a church had to wait for popular subscription to get a frame building, 36 by 58 feet.

Indian troubles ended with the surrender of Old John, one of the main trouble makers, the last chief to come to the treaty grounds on the Rogue River. He set his gun against a rock during negotiations

UPPER FLOOR of grist mill had V-shaped floor, divided by partition, bottom on each side having opening for chute through which either of two kinds of grain could be fed to grinding stones. These photos were made in spring of 1963 when historic mill was due to be burned. Dam in river remains, impounded pool still providing neighboring children with swimming hole.

risings. The land was at the southern end of the town of Kings Valley and belonged to Rowland Chambers who sold it willingly enough.

At the rear of the bench and set against the hill was the largest building, the barracks. Immediately to the left was the latrine, then the commissary, water tower and bakery. The guard house was placed at the right of the barracks and farther down, near the foot of the bench, a hospital with Dr. D. G. Campbell of Corvallis in charge. The building still stands. At the left of it were the several buildings serving as officers' quarters which completed the square. In the center was a spacious parade ground.

Lt. Philip Sheridan, active in the Oregon wars in 1859, was the first in charge of Fort Hoskins but he was soon promoted to higher rank in the Civil War which followed. Taking his place was Capt. Augur, the unfortunate who had to take the brunt of complaints from neighboring farmers as to the behavior of his soldiers. One such protest was strongly worded. "The garrison at Fort Hoskins has a strong predilection for wine, women and song. Details are so indelicate they will not bear repeating." The report obviously lacked the savory details some wanted but ended with the definite statement: "The soldiers are a menace to the peace and prosperity of the community."

The captain is reported to have been "upset". He wrote letters to the farmers and neighbors ranging from Kings Valley itself to the little town on the other side of the fort called Fort Hoskins requesting

and at one point grabbed it to shoot down the officer reading the terms. When fifty soldiers aimed their rifles at him he gave up, temporarily, and surrendered his weapon. He was first sent with other Indians to the reservation at Grande Ronde, northeast of Kings Valley. When the neighboring farmers complained "the ground here is too good to waste on redskins. They ought to be thrown out so we can farm it", the Indians were transferred to the Siletz agency, farther south and near the Coast. A fort was ordered built at the western gate of the reservation, not so much to protect the settlers from the Indians as to guard the natives from being debauched by the whites. In this lofty aim the authorities were not entirely successful.

The site selected for Fort Hoskins was on a bench of a gently rising hill overlooking the lower part of the Luckiamute Valley, beautifully serene but considered the most likely spot for Indian up-

ROWLAND CHAMBERS with some of brood. Picture is thin, positive film on cracked glass, provided some problems in copying by this photographer. It is about 100 years old.

FAMILY GATHERING photo was taken after Rowland Chambers passed away but not before he had started population explosion. First wife died on journey to Oregon, second probably woman at right of infant in center, eldest daughter at left. Relationship of others vague. Many now rest in old Kings Valley cemetery not far away.

them to state their feelings on the matter. As reports came in Augur held a plebiscite with Rowland Chambers, L. Norton, O. King — son of the late Nahum — and other parties concerned. The somewhat surprising consensus was stated: "Either the farmers have had a change of heart or else the chief complainant, Mr. Ross Browne, was a liar." True, one farmer did say that although he had made good money selling the soldiers milk and eggs, the profit was nullified by their thefts of his hogs which they butchered and added to the commissary as a change of diet.

There was also continual trouble from Indians who insisted on coming over from the Siletz reservation and getting into trouble with the white settlers. One was caught peeking into the bedroom window of a farm house. The owner swore he would kill the next Indian Peeping Tom and he promptly did. This caused an uproar but the bereaved family was quickly placated with a payment of $200 by the army.

Then there was the incident concerning the beautiful Indian girl and young Lieutenant Garber. On duty at Fort Hoskins, he became acquainted with the girl in the early spring of 1850. She was soon visiting the reputedly "very handsome" officer in his quarters and then moving in, apparently tolerated by fellow officers until her parents complained, not so much on moral grounds as they needed her at home. Hoping to put an end to the affair, Augur sent Garber to Fort Vancouver to cool off, but reckoned without the persistence of the young squaw who walked all the way to the fort on the Columbia River to rejoin her lover. Garber was returned to Fort Hoskins and brought before Captain Augur for a dressing down and a warning to stop seeing the girl. This was supposed to end the matter but the Indian maiden was again discovered in the lieutenant's rooms. Again sent for by Augur, tempers flared on both sides and Garber made some insubordinate remarks. He was sentenced to six months in the guard house but died of unstated causes in a few months. He was buried in the Kings Valley cemetery, his grave identified only by the regular army marker for a time. Then his fellow soldiers contributed funds for a marble marker which stands today. Ironically, as though pointing up his ill luck, his name is misspelled.

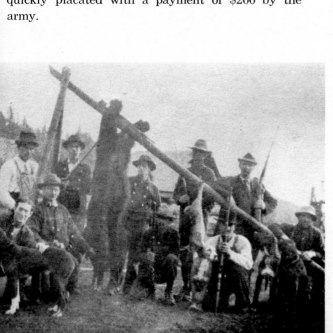

OCCASIONAL BEAR was killed by soldiers and civilians at Fort Hoskins. Comment of one soldier: "It was a treat to get something we could eat once in a while." This and other very old pictures were loaned by descendant of Rowland Chambers.

OLD BLACKSMITH SHOP still stands on Fort Hoskins grounds. It is complete with forge and monstrous, hand-operated bellows, making intense heat for horse shoes and metal equipment. Fort is on private land requiring permission for visit.

FRAME BUILDING now occupied by private family was once Fort Hoskins hospital. Although altered and preserved, it is essentially same as original with many obviously old details in interior construction. Author's visit was made in spring, evidenced by cherry blossoms.

CHITWOOD, OREGON

Grace Davis left her telephone switchboard only once. It taught her a stern lesson. Now Mrs. Collins of Portland she thinks back to 1906, to her life in the rugged, timbered mountains of the Oregon coast.

There were only about twenty telephone subscribers but their calls kept Grace Davis busy almost the whole twenty-four hours she was on duty. Although she loved the job there were jangling interruptions while she was busy with other necessary duties that "got on her nerves" some days. This one day she made up her mind she would finish her lunch, buzzing or no buzzing. She tried to shut her ears until she finished eating and then sweetly answered the signal.

The voice was that of Chauncey Trapp, conductor of the eastbound train, telling her it had been wrecked below Chitwood and he had been trying to get her for fifteen minutes and he was about crazy, that she must get out there and stop the westbound train when it passed through Chitwood to avoid a terrible collision. Grace jumped and barely had time to warn the engineer as the train was pulling out. "That was the only time I ever ignored the switchboard," Grace says now. "And I haven't really felt safe in telling the story until now, almost sixty years later."

The area was a primeval wilderness in the 1860s when M. L. Trapp and his wife settled on a land claim a short distance below where the town would be. Life was lonely for the solitary woman until the Barney Morrisons took the next location. In a few more years more hardy pioneers came to cut the trees and till the soil. Some had families, more children were born and the need for a school arose. A house with one large room a half mile west of Chitwood was pressed into service, a fireplace at one end being the only source of heat. No one seemed to have time to cut firewood of proper length so the teacher, Thomas J. Brannan, poked the ends of large branches in the blaze and moved them farther in as they burned. There were no desks or tables so the pupils sat on benches and did their sums on slates in their laps.

After a few years of hardships some of the settlers gave up and moved away, taking their children with them, so education languished for a while. Then Mr. Trapp, one of the persistent ones, offered the use of a room in his home and hired a teacher who "lived in."

It was not until 1887 that a real school was built, its location near Chitwood and built by donated labor. It became the center for all community affairs — box socials, committee meetings, farm group get-togethers, Christmas parties and even weddings. Sometimes itinerant evangelists would hold revival meetings in the little "hall". A collection of books donated by residents, became the nucleus of a growing library shortly after the turn of the century and the "hello girl," Grace Davis, served as librarian.

During the early years many adherents of the Seventh Day Adventist faith wanted a church which could double as a school, but lumber was scarce and the dream had to be postponed. Then a little farm building in nearby Elk City which was already fading was dismantled and the material hauled to Chitwood by a sturdy pair of oxen—Lep and Lion. Lep was conspicuously spotted and was first called Leopard until it proved cumbersome. Oxen were best for hauling on the deeply rutted, muddy roads, but their doom was spelled when at last the railroad came—and with it P. A. Miller.

He had been Per Anderson in Sweden but that country's army complained there were already too many Andersons and would Per please change his name? The young Swede borrowed one of his cousin's and became Per Moeller. After the army service he took his new bride, Marie, to Chitwood and they lived in a section house while the Corvallis and Eastern Railroad was being built. And his name got "in the road" again. His daughter Lillie tells about it. "My father was quick to embrace new ideas, new things. As soon as he realized his name was awkward to American tongues he abbreviated Per to P, then inserted an A for the original Anderson and simplified Moeller to Miller. For the rest of his life he was P. A. Miller."

He was soon transferred to Mill City in the Willamette Valley at the very edge of the Cascade Mountains and helped build some of the bridges for frequent crossings of the Santiam River which

TRACKS OF CORVALLIS AND EASTERN, later branch line of Southern Pacific, run close by old George Smith store at right. Line ran from Corvallis in Willamette Valley over Coast Range to Yaquina on bay of same name, connecting agricultural area to coast, was started in 1880. Trains were first composed of flat car or two, a few box cars and about three coaches, hauled by puffing, wood-burning engine. Number of farmers added to income by cutting fuel on private wood lots, stacking it beside track. When train crew saw a pile ready, they would stop train and load it on tender. Passenger service was finally discontinued, tracks taken up between Yaquina and Toledo. Covered bridge is 96 feet long, was built in early 1920s, replacing hand-hewn span.

SNOW IS RARE in coastal area of Oregon, helps to delineate buildings shown in picture made about 1900. At extreme left is store built by Lafayette Pepin, rented to Rogers two years, then run by Pepin. Next right is old bridge of hand-hewn beams, above it Seventh Day Adventist Church. Large house with surrounding porch was originally owned by Mr. Durkee, later housing telephone office and switchboard, and still stands but long unoccupied. Next right is post office, shown in modern photo without porch. Next is railway depot, back of that old Whitney store, later operated by George Smith. Above is old Chitwood family home. Forest fire nearly denuded hills now covered with luxurious growth.

twisted down its narrow canyon. But he was dissatisfied because the job kept him away from home where his young wife was expecting her first child. He applied for the job of track maintenance on the Chitwood line where he could have permanent residence with his family. His request was granted six months after the baby girl was born, so the little family moved to a train stop called Morrison Station just below Chitwood, close enough for Lillie to go to school when ready.

Young Miller did well at his job and managed to improve his small home too but with the birth of two sons he started building a much larger one. Lillie's memories really begin with this house. "It had lots of bedrooms and a huge kitchen with a big wood range. Just above it, on the side of the steep hill was a woodshed which seemed as large as the house and appeared attached to it. One of the many people who stopped with my folks remarked: 'This

is the first time I ever saw a two-story woodshed'. There was always company at our house, salesman or drummer, itinerant preacher and, of course the school teacher. Everyone seemed to think it was expected he stay with the Millers, and mother, on whom the largest share of the extra work fell, never protested although it must have seemed she was running a boarding house."

The wagon road was a sea of mud in winter, with dust a foot deep in summer. Much later when the first automobiles began to filter in, it was said: "One car would raise so much dust that another couldn't follow it for a long time." In the muddy season the road was completely impassable but this did not handicap the section foreman. He had access to a hand car — a tiny, four-wheeled platform that ran on rails, powered by a handle bar worked up and down. It was a back-breaking job for one man but was easier when two used the rig, one facing forward and one backward, each man alternately lowering and raising the handles like the operation of a see-saw.

Just as the patient Mrs. Miller was relied upon to "put up" all stray visitors, so was P. A. trusted to take care of any emergency such as fetching the doctor when someone was desperately ill or an imminent childbirth. When called upon he would jump on the hand car and pump madly to Elk City where the doctor lived and with that worthy's help on the other end of the handle, speed to wherever needed. Since most of these calls came at night when the trains did not run, there was little danger on the rails. When Elk City declined and could no longer maintain a doctor, Miller was forced to pump his rig all the way to Toledo.

The right of way ignored most of the twistings of the Yaquina River along which it was built with spidery trestles and tunnels through projecting points of rock. When Lillie started going to school in Chitwood, she and other children walked the ties to avoid the muddy road. "We got very expert at hurrying over the trestles," she says, "so as not to be on one when a train came." In a year or two she was joined on the walk by her little brother whose twin had died in infancy.

Coming home from school one day the children came to a pile of glowing embers where the section crew had been burning old ties. The children put more wood on the dying fire and fanned it to a blaze. As Lillie stooped low over the flames her dress caught fire. In a panic she ran back to the school house and fortunately the teacher was still there. She tore most of the clothes from the little girl's body and rolled her in a coat. Lillie was a long time recovering from her burns, the scars still showing faintly.

It was about this period that a "prospector" from San Francisco discovered a fine vein of sandstone nearby, the material deemed most suitable for construction of the mint and post office in his home city. The Corvallis and Eastern ran a spur line into the quarry, the sandstone cut and loaded by hand on flat cars hauled to Yaquina, the lower terminus on Yaquina Bay, and trans-shipped on vessels to San Francisco. The industry caused quite an influx of workers for a time, "inflating" the tiny community to some extent.

In 1905 a movement was started for a telephone line to serve Chitwood, P. A. Miller in particular feeling the telegraph was not adequate. It was his responsibility to see that the long stretch of track was kept in good repair and he needed better communi-

cations with those who lived along the route. So on December 14, 1905, the Rural Telephone Co. was organized with A. L. McDonald as chairman, George T. Smith as secretary-treasurer. The list of signed members starts with P. A. Miller, includes most of the responsible residents including the Pepins, Wilsons, the younger Trapp and W. N. Cook. The office and switchboard was set up in the Durky house, owned by Miss Jean Robertson. It was here Grace Davis took over as switchboard operator. At first the line went only to Morrison Station but was soon expanded and eventually connected to the outside world for long distance calls, at first a big thrill for Grace Davis.

The coming of the Corvallis and Eastern changed things for Chitwood more than any other factor. When travel was confined to the wagon road, the stages sometimes got through and sometimes did not. The first fall rains turned the heavy dust into a quagmire in which wagons and stages were bogged down to the hubs.

CHITWOOD POST OFFICE was for years in George Smith store with Smith as postmaster. Later it was transferred to this little building. After it was closed out, door was enlarged and building served as garage. This business also has gone but pigeon-hole racks still hang on walls where they held letters. Huge chestnut tree once shaded front, was cut down some years ago, new growth springing up, as shown here in bloom.

When stages did get through they were useful. A man with a freshly killed deer carcass who lacked flour could wrap up a hind quarter in a sack, take the stage to Corvallis, make a trade in the store and return by stage with his flour.

When the puffing, wood-burners started pulling trains from Corvallis to Yaquina, Chitwood became an important stop. The little depot was close by George Smith's store and post office and train time always stirred the town into a frenzy. Grace Davis, in addition to her switchboard and library, saw that the mail sack was thrown on board, the incoming one taken off.

Since George Smith was the butcher as well as grocer there was always a smelly bale of cowhides ready for shipping. There would be sacks of dried and crushed cascara bark gathered in the woods where the trees abounded and carried out in bundles strapped to the pickers' backs. Cord upon cord of wood would be stacked beside the tracks for train crews to load as fuel for the boiler. Cutters got 90 cents a cord delivered on right-of-way. And trains brought large shipments of goods for George Smith's store.

The store had its beginnings in a small building put up by Joshua Chitwood who served as first postmaster as well, selling out later to a Mr. Whitney. George Smith worked in the store and later married the owner's daughter, taking over ownership after Whitney's retirement.

You could buy anything you needed at George's store. If it was not on hand it would be "sent for" from Corvallis and come in on the train. Bee keeping was an important part of the economy, Smith himself having an apiary and selling his neighbors a complete line of supplies, hives, supers and even queens on occasion. He sold meat but allowed customers to use his facilities for their own slaughtering.

Growing up and going to school here was Smith's son Morris. When he was old enough to work he did many jobs and then at 24 was elated to get steady work at another, later stone quarry. The stone was regularly blasted out of the solid vein by chipping out a "coyote" hole, placing the charge, then plugging up the hole with tapered rock with the wide ends out so they would jam tightly with the explosion, causing the full force of the blast to go upward instead of out the hole. Morris had gone to the cook shack for lunch one day which had been delayed for the scheduled twelve o'clock blast. This time a shower of badly placed rocks arched high overhead and came hurtling down through the roof of the shack, pinning Morris to the floor by his leg, crushing it from the ankle to above the knee. After a year of hospitalization, the knee was left rigid and ankle almost so.

GAY TIMES WERE HAD in olden days at Chitwood's dance hall.

When Morris left the hospital he found the depression in full swing. With few jobs available he was happy when his father offered to take him into the store and as he kept busy, the leg improved. He cultivated berries and orchard fruit near the store, sold the produce there or with honey to the coast resorts at Newport.

When Lillie Miller graduated from the Chitwood grade school she went to high school in Toledo, thirteen miles away. It was hard to get there and lonely staying there so after the first year she took courses at home. When ready she taught in several of the small area schools and saving her money, took a summer course at Oregon Agricultural College at Corvallis, western terminus of Corvallis and Eastern. She had a stint of teaching at West Linn across the Willamette from Oregon City, graduating from the University of Oregon at Eugene. After a few years she married Charles A. Nutt and moved to Portland where she now lives, a widow.

When the old wagon road was rerouted and paved the improvement was hailed in Chitwood as a great thing. Automobiles, coming rapidly into popularity, used the new, short route to the coast. Soon no one was riding the train and with increasingly large tonnage of freight shipped by truck, the railroad reduced service to a minimum, discontinuing passenger service. The depot was torn down and many people moved away. Business was so slow at the Pepin and Smith stores, now that larger stores and markets were so readily reached by automobile, both owners quit trying. Chitwood, although retaining a few residents who love the place, is now a virtual ghost.

ELK CITY, OREGON

Mary's Peak is the most prominent mountain in the Coast Range as it crosses Benton County. Down its western slope flows a clear, sparkling stream typical of those in coastal Oregon. Near its banks, in 1856, was camped a party of explorers in search of grazing land. Food supplies were low and supper was expected to be beans as usual. Then one man saw a fine bull elk standing on a hill, an easy mark for his gun. In memory of this provident event the stream became Elk Creek.

About four years later, where this stream flows into the Yaquina River, a small settlement grew up. It was named Newton for the man who laid out the plat, Albitha Newton, and placed it as far up the Yaquina as boats could go. During normal low water periods the stream was quite narrow, branches hanging low and sometimes brushing the heads of boat passengers. Water-soaked snags lurked on the bottom of the none too deep waterway to scrape bottoms or rip holes in them. At times of high water the menace of low trees and branches became worse but the influence of ocean tides became noticeable.

As Newton grew and more travel came up the river from Toledo, Yaquina and Newport below on the bay, efforts were made to clear the waterway by removing snags and cutting branches. A small dock was prefabricated at Toledo, brought up on a barge and installed on the bank. Then it was possible for small steamboats to tie up at the town and regular service was instituted. A flat-bottomed stern wheeler was the first to make regular runs, down the bay one day and back the next. The railroad was also completed through Newton and on to bay points.

Two saloons, a hotel, store, Odd Fellows Lodge which was shared by other fraternal orders, many cabins and houses — all grew up on the site, giving the place the appearance of a real town.

The first post office had been established in 1868 with E. A. Abbey the postmaster. Marshall Simpson held the job next, was out of the office for a while and then returned November 23, 1888. He came full of ideas about advancing the status of the little town and one of the first efforts he made was getting the name changed from Newton to Elk City to conform to the name of the post office.

The town flourished until automobiles took away the need for river traffic. And as logging in the area declined so did Elk City. Another blow was the abandonment of the rock quarries which had provided a live industry with workers living and buying supplies in the town.

The old grocery which for years housed the post office is the only business still going in the town by the Yaquina. The Scovilles now operate it and a gas pump. They tell of frequent floods when the only traffic through the main street was by boat. "All these coastal rivers are short," says Mr. Scoville. "Our heavy winter rains of sometimes two and three inches a day quickly swell them to flood heights. In early days there was a sawmill and hotel here. One time when the river was exceptionally high the water took a lot of lumber piled in the sawmill yard and slammed it against the hotel, turning it on its side so it had to be torn down. It was never rebuilt and neither was the wrecked sawmill. That seems to be the way the old town went, little by little."

Elk City still has at least one resource, says Mr. Scoville. "We have extra good fishing here, especially in the middle of summer when steelhead salmon and blueback are running. Then fishermen bring their families over from the Willamette Valley and stay a while. We keep those little cabins there rented all the time."

PICTURESQUE COVERED BRIDGE once carried passenger traffic to depot which still stands on other side but falling into ruin. Spanning Yaquina River it is almost smothered under dense vegetation typical of Oregon coastal country. Town is only three miles in air line from Toledo, largest town in area, nine miles by river, only means of access at one time. Elk City's covered bridge, built about 1922, is 100 feet long.

KERNVILLE, OREGON

All that glitters in ghost town lore is not gold. It can even be the silver horde Rex Beach wrote about — the silvery sides of salmon establishing an industry and a town. It happened that way at Kernville.

The man who started it was Daniel Kern, born in Menominee, Michigan, on September 12, 1856. He came west at twenty-one, working at one odd job after another in Portland, Oregon. They taught him how to get along with people and lead them and in a short time he was a contractor on jetty projects at the mouth of the Columbia River, at Bandon, Coos Bay, Yaquina, and Grays Harbor on the Washington coast. Kern was particular about the type of rock used in the jetties and prospected for the material personally. He discovered the quarry at Elk City, Oregon, and the sandstone from it was sent down the Yaquina River to build the breakwater in the bay.

A man working along the Washington and Oregon coasts in those days could not help being involved with salmon in one way or another. In

OLD BUSINESS CENTER of Millport, as Kernville was confusingly called in hectic days of first world war, surrounded by stranded and neglected fishing boats. Building in background housed general offices of mill company. Beyond, now collapsed, were bunkhouses called "bachelors' halls." Fish boat on side is typical of thousands plying coastal rivers, most of them in war years equipped with famous Regal engines. Two-man crews laid out gill nets across stream and let them drift with current, catching whatever type of salmon was running, with sturgeon and other fish.

1896, Dan Kern enlisted his brother, John H., as partner and built a large fish cannery on the north bank of the Oregon coastal river called the Siletz. Wildly remote from civilization, the spot became the first white settlement in North Lincoln County.

Two years later a youth, Warren Pohle of Salem, took a trip to the coast to fish the Siletz. He later wrote — "The river was full of Indians fishing for salmon to supply the cannery there." He said the Indians got 25¢ apiece for Chinooks and a dime for "silversides", regardless of size. The Kern Bros. Packing Co. was later sold to Mat P. Kiernan and J. W. Cooke of Portland and eventually Sam Elmore of Astoria took it over.

Elmore wrecked the building, using the lumber to rebuild a short distance from the Siletz. The "new" Elmore Cannery employed a large number of Chinese laborers in the plant, bunkhouses being built back of the main building. Rice was their staple food, imported by the ton, the straw bundles coming in by boat. Eventually the cannery became a boat building plant.

Elections were held in the cannery, the precinct being called "Kern." A number of other industries, including a sawmill, were developed on the south side of the small river, the short crossing made by boat. The post office was also established there, July 6, 1896, with John Kern as the first postmaster, succeeded by Mat Kiernan. There were some dark, slack periods in Kernville history when the post office was listed as "Not In Service."

Daniel's daughter Grace, who now lives in retirement in Portland, recalls a trip to Kernville in the early days before there was a road along the coast. "We spent a summer at the cannery, hoping the sea air would be of benefit to my brother Arthur who was suffering from rheumatic fever. I was two years younger but well remember the interesting trip from Portland. We went to Corvallis, transfering to a line called the Corvallis and Eastern. It was pulled by a wood-burning locomotive and ran only to Yaquina on the coast. We got off at Toledo just this side of Yaquina and again transferred, this time to a buckboard. We rode on this to a place called Olsen's Landing, then completed the remainder of the trip to the Siletz by rowboat. There

were four young men there on a fishing trip, one of them a medical student named Lee Steiner. All the young men had beautiful voices and would serenade us every night. Then one day Arthur had a very bad attack of the fever. Mr. Steiner carried him to the salmon boat which was to get us to the steamer for Astoria and he stayed with us, helping mother take care of Arthur. At Astoria we got on the train going up the Oregon side of the Columbia River to Portland where we met my father who took us to the hospital there. My brother recovered and about 1943 met Dr. Steiner who remarked — "You don't look much like the sick boy I carried out of Kernville years ago."

Kernville's busiest years were those when Kaiser Wilhelm was so close to winning the First World War. Oregon's coastal spruce was found to be the best material known for making airplanes. The Sitka spruce reached its finest development and heaviest stand along the lower Siletz. An average acre of these trees yielded 150,000 board feet. A sawmill, the Kernville Spruce Division Mill, with a capacity of 30,000 feet a day had to "hump it" to cope with the War Department's estimate of 3 billion board feet accessible from tidewater. The mill maintained a schedule with creditable consistency, considering all the difficulties of production. There was no dependable wagon road reaching the place. Wet weather made a quagmire of the only road there was and high tides covered it. The Siletz was crossed by a "drift and pull" ferry, since no bridge had been built, and this river was only one of many along the route north.

Except for a few supplies brought in by wagon in the summer when roads were dryer and tides lower, all materials depended upon boat shipments and there were plenty of troubles with these too. The depth of the Siletz bar was only about seven feet in a changing channel.

When a drawbridge was finally completed over the Siletz in November of 1926, it was a major link in the coastal highway system, so impeded with tidal flats, rivers and canyons. Kernville was already a ghost town and the new bridge only hastened the removal of almost all the remaining residents and old machinery from the mill to the new Kernville on the highway.

OLD LANDING DOCK at Kernville was on south bank of Siletz. Cannery was opposite, later converted to boat building plant which is still operating. Short distance upstream is Coyote Rock, basaltic projection partly blocking river. Name stems from Indian legend. Coyote was tribal deity, god of food and plenty, who spent time fishing for salmon and conceived idea of building dam across stream to trap them and simplify job. He was throwing rocks in water when another god, Sea Lion, stopped him, saying salmon could not get upstream to spawn if river was obstructed. Coyote desisted but left partially completed dam at edge.

GLENCO, WYOMING

Were there a hundred hardy, enterprising young men available who would go on a trapping expedition for three years? General William Ashley hoped so. He and partner Andrew Henry planned a foray into the Rocky Mountain wilderness and to attract men, advertised in MISSOURI REPUBLICAN of March 20, 1822.

Plenty of men wanted to go. In three weeks Ashley had his hundred lined up and ready to start on the great adventure. The "Ashley-Henry Men" included many who would become famous mountain guides and scouts, such as young Jim Bridger, Jedediah Smith and the four Sublette brothers.

The expedition and further explorations were to have a heavy impact on the history of Wyoming and the West, opening the South Pass route to Oregon, navigating the Green River, discovering and navigating Great Salt Lake. It was while crossing from the Green to Salt Lake that the party discovered the coal outcroppings along Ham's Fork of the Green River and Ashley reported: "The coal sticks out of the ground in places and would seem to extend vast distances underground." The general was never to know just how right he was for it was 72 years later that the Ham's Fork district was opened to mining at Diamondville near Kemmerer.

Patrick J. Quealy, coal inspector for the Union Pacific Railroad, interested Mahlon S. Kemmerer of Pennsylvania in organizing the Kemmerer Coal Mining Co., founding the town of Kemmerer and thus starting the vast network of mines in the immediate area. Six years later the mine superintendent of one of these, Diamond Coke and Fuel Co. made a strike in "black gold" on a little prospecting trip of his own.

He was Thomas Sneddon, a Scot not long from the old country. He came to Ham's Fork hoping to start a mine of his own but took a job with the Diamond Co. and did some private prospecting. Southeast of Diamondville he stumbled upon just such an outcropping of coal as Gen. Ashley had described, made a claim, quit his job and started

the mine he had dreamed of. Its name had been in mind ever since leaving Scotland — the little town of Glencoe. As the coal mines developed and the miners needed a town nearer than Diamondville, Sneddon laid out a street running south from the sage-covered hills, sold real estate on both sides for stores and named the new town Glencoe also.

Miners were imported from all parts of the country and foreign ones as well. Their work was hard and dangerous, especially as the slanting shafts penetrated thousands of feet into the hills. They wore kerosene lamps on their caps for feeble illumination and there was the everpresent danger of explosion from black damp. The work was of the heaviest kind, mostly done in winter, and the pay was by the ton, $3 for a ten hour day being about as much as the strongest miner could earn. Coal was hauled out of the stopes by mules in the early days, then freighted down to the railroad by wagons.

Homes were crude, some of boards, more mere dugouts or partially excavated holes extended with slabs of rock or wood. They had the advantage of being warmer in the bitter Wyoming winters when temperatures sagged to thirty below and winds sifted snow through every crack.

Frank Scigliano, now of Kemmerer, was born in Glencoe in 1936. The town was then going down hill fast, the family moving away when Frank was six. He gives a vivid picture of the death throes of the town. "My first memories of Glencoe are of the one street lined on both sides by false-fronted buildings. They were pretty decrepit, I guess, as I think of them now, but they looked pretty grand to me then. I remember our family used to talk often of the terrible explosions in other mines, especially the one in 1927, when 100 men were killed in the Frontier mine and another at Sublet where 39 were killed. Most of the women worried all day while their men were underground. My mother often said she wished father would find some other kind of work than mining but he didn't know anything else. Then one day we heard that awful, ruffled rumble. Smoke belched out of the mouth of the mine,

WALLS OF DUGOUT HOME are partly of native earth, partly of four feet thick stones. Such houses were warmer than those entirely above ground. "Front yard" is naturally landscaped with ubiquitous sage brush, sharply delineated in late afternoon side-lighting.

FLAT, NATURALLY SPLIT SHALE ROCKS were available in quantity for building, though no house was built entirely of this native material, likely because wind would penetrate even several thicknesses of uneven slabs. Winters were cruelly cold at Glencoe but plenty of coal was available for fuel, prevailing bituminous grade yielding ample heat. Anthracite, generally credited only to old mines at Cambria, was also found at Glencoe, brought too good a price to be used at home.

RUINS OF GLENCOE are few enough, scattered over wide area. Houses, never solidly built, are either in state of collapse or have disappeared entirely. One in foreground of photo was built of slabs and heavy, hand-hewn beams, dates from early stages of town. Other scattered shacks are from later periods.

mother started to scream, then got hold of herself and joined the other women at the shaft. All they could do was wait. When the smoke and fumes cleared away the rescuers began to bring out survivors. Each man was greeted in turn by his wife, but then the men who were carrying them out told all the women to go home. Those women whose men hadn't been brought out knew the terrible truth. It was only then that they broke down and cried, all of them, the ones whose husbands had been saved and the others. My father had been one of the first to be rescued. He said the dust, smoke and confusion was so bad the rescuers were nearly overcome too. I think eight men lost their lives in that explosion."

The disaster, coupled with the fact that the coal was giving out, caused the closing of the mines. In the early 1940s everybody moved away, most of the miners going to work in the Brilliant and Elko mines. "I didn't know it then, but I heard later that the closing of the Glencoe meant finish to another town just below. It was called Bon Rico. There were two saloons there and a dancehall where there were lots of girls. I used to hear my father joke about going 'down to Bon Rico to have some fun' and I never knew why mother always flared up and said it wasn't funny. Actually, I think that the days when the girls earned a living at Bon Rico were gone before we lived at Glencoe. There were some pretty wild times there in the old days though."

OPAL, WYOMING

WYOMING'S OPAL
A PROGRESSIVE WESTERN TOWN
IN UINTA COUNTY

More cattle, sheep and wool shipped from that point each season than in any other town in the state.

So headlined a lead article in the Cheyenne DAILY LEADER of July 10, 1895. The writer continued:

"The following interesting story is obtained from the impression made on the mind of an eastern newspaper representative while visiting Opal, a thriving town in Uinta County: Scattered on either side of a heavy upgrade of the Union Pacific tracks, leading from a canyon of the Uinta Mountains of Wyoming, are some half a dozen log houses, a saloon and as many corrals. This is Opal. It seems the height of impudence, writes a tenderfoot correspondent of the Philadelphia Inquirer, that a town so limited in its proportions should occupy a place on the map, but Opal is an important city.

"For that matter, a section house, a sidetracked handcar and a signboard are all that are required to make up a western "city" and a guaranteed license to appear on the map, and in the very same size type as any of its sister cities.

"Opal, with its half dozen houses is a metropolis. It is a railroad center for a district covering 200 miles to the north, embracing a region of sheep and cattle ranches among the wealthiest in Wyoming and the newly discovered gold mines at Cora, the hope of thousands of speculators and miners.

"Opal has many advantages, it is away up, resting some 7,400 feet above the sea level. Then there

CABLE SPOOL, one of many relics of days of 1920s scattered along banks of Ham's Fork of Green River. Natural oil seepages around Opal and most of Wyoming were known and used for medicinal and lubricating purposes from earliest times. Big demand came with automobiles and probings for oil extended into every corner of Wyoming, opening both rich fields and "dusters." The holes drilled at Opal proved the latter type but enough oil was discovered at nearby La Barge to cause boom in '20s, the town calling itself Tulsa for a time. After bubble burst, abashed townspeople again used name of La Barge, from nearby La Barge Creek, that named in 1824 by General Ashley for friend Joseph La Barge. Opal, at first envious of oil discovery at La Barge, was glad to escape similar fate.

COMMUNITY WATER TANK dates back to Opal's busy days as sheep and cattle shipping center, is still in use for few remaining residents.

is plenty of room and no crowded streets. Four horse teams or bunches of cattle pass each other in the busiest thoroughfare without coming within speaking distance of each other. The only government building in the place is the postoffice which occupies a corner of the little station, while the noticeable absence of jails and police stations strengthens the air of freedom which characterizes this western town.

"The Opalites are as interesting as the place they live in. The man who owns the store is the acknowledged mayor of the city He is not elected to that high office. He doesn't need to be. His position demands it and thrown into contact with every man on the entire range he hears all their troubles while putting up their orders, and is broad minded enough to agree with all, one at a time. In this way he is the confidant of every customer and if he occasionally or invariably charges for a half hour's sympathy in connection with a side of pork, no objection is made.

"The store-keeper at Opal is not only recognized to be, but naturally is, the cleverest man in the place. He is just what the successful western store-keeper must be, a first class business man, a hustler, a true judge of human nature and always to be relied upon in time of trouble, a clever entertainer, cool, courageous, and all in all a man embracing all the true and genuine qualities of that intricately constructed animal. Just such a man is the store-keeper at Opal. Always on the alert to make a dollar, he is quite as quick to drive all night with a doctor from some of the neighboring cities to be at the bedside of a suffering rancher. If he is quick to charge a man coming to the store in possession of his full health he is just as quick to forget to charge a man who is sick or in any trouble. There is an unprinted ordinance in Opal to the effect that 'This is a country where you get nothing for nothing, and damn little for a nickel' but in sickness or real distress the westerner is the quickest to see the wants of his neighbor or any man in the world, and he gives assistance in a roughly delicate way that does not make the receiver read 'charity' in anything he gives him.

"As implied by its name, Opal is very rich in minerals and precious stones, it is from this place that the wonderful specimens sold at Manitou and other Colorado resorts as peculiar phenomena and natural formations of the hot springs are first shipped. Although these curiosities come from the Town of Opal, the town derives no revenue from their sale. The specimens are common property and are to be had for the picking.

In a business way this little town near the Utah line of Wyoming is an example of western push and enterprise. Each year more than 10,000 cattle are shipped to Chicago, as many sheep and one quarter of a million pounds of wool to Philadelphia and other eastern markets. In return supplies for the hundreds of ranches in the north country are sent here for distribution and about the little station there is always a burly crowd of teamsters as there is at the Broadway Depot, even if the number is smaller and of a different kind. Altogether, Opal is a typical western city, a place where the chase after the almighty dollar supersedes the chase after the soft and scented anise-seed bag as a form of entertainment, and the possession of gold is the one ambition of everyman's life."

Opal, along with many other towns stretching across southern Wyoming, owed its birth to the building of the railroads. As Union Pacific rails penetrated west from Cheyenne in the 1860s, shacks, barracks and makeshift restaurants were set up at intervals. Hastily erected saloons, dance halls and various dives were thrown together in ramshackle haste to cater to rail workers. When the tracks had progressed a sufficient distance beyond, all portable company buildings were moved to the new location and again set up. Hanger-on enterprises followed suit, wrecking their flimsy structures and rebuilding where the business was. A large transient population thus moved along with the railhead, surveyors, graders, contractors, track layers and other workers connected with the road building, followed by some reputable business men, and a large proportion of riff-raff. These wild, traveling towns were full of what was called "Hell-on-wheels." Most of them vanished utterly away with the moving on of the tracks, leaving little visible evidence of a lusty interlude. Others would hang on for a time before giving up, others developed into permanence because of having some sort of back ground furnishing goods for shipping, nearby coal fields or oil deposits.

The usual boom camp sprouted at the junction point, called Granger. For a time the population ran into a thousand or so. Three box cars on a siding provided a railway station. The first one was the freight depot, the next was the ticket office and baggage section. The third did duty as waiting room. Men's and Ladies' lounges were divided by a chalk line across the middle, the men were allowed to smoke on their own side, only.

The UP line turned sharply southwestward at Granger, a point west of Rock Springs, heading for Ogden and Salt Lake City, and for a long time the area to the northwest with its rich potential of coal and oil lay without transportation. Then, in 1889 the Utah and Northern built a narrow gauge line through it, connecting to the UP. This line was later called the Oregon Short Line, still later consolidating with UP. The line also had its traveling towns on a smaller scale, one of these remaining permanently as Opal because of the good watering place at Ham's Fork of Green River. So Opal became a flourishing shipping point for livestock. Also, the place was subjected to periods of oil excitement, none of which amounted to anything solid for Opal, although tremendously booming the state as a whole.

There were many seeps of high quality petroleum in the area. Indians had been using the liquid from prehistoric times as an ointment or salve for tired and sore limbs. Early white settlers expanded the liquid's uses by pouring it over dried buffalo chips, making a quick starting fuel. In 1849 Mormons and California-bound gold seekers passing through Uinta County mixed oil with flour as a grease for axles. During the 1860s and '70s much exploratory oil-well drilling was done in Uinta County. Several attempts to find the fluid were made in Opal itself, none of which were successful, but each period of drilling was accompanied by wildest speculation and excitement, all of which would die down as the hole turned out a "duster."

It was during one of these temporary booms that the following incident was reported, also on the CHEYENNE DAILY LEADER. "A ranchman applied for lodging at the section house, operated by a woman. He was accommodated, and when he went to bed he left under his pillow his money, a considerable sum. In the morning he left his room, forgetting to take his money with him. Later he remembered it, and rushing back found the landlady making the bed. He asked her for his purse. She said she knew nothing about it. He was sure she had it and finally caught her by the arm and demanded his money. She screamed, and a lot of men hearing her rushed in, and thinking the man had insulted her, hung him from the nearest telegraph pole without giving him a chance to explain. It was later found that the woman had stolen the money, but beneath that same telegraph pole lies buried an innocent man."

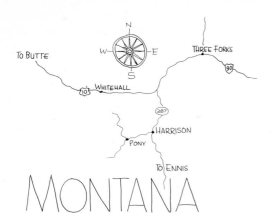

PONY, MONTANA

He was less than five feet tall, his accomplishments in proportion. Few people noticed him as he moved from creek to creek, panning enough gold to keep him in beans and get him to the next camp. In 1866 he was crowded out of Alder Gulch and Virginia City by bigger men and made his lonely way to the far-out edges of Tobacco Root Range.

Here in a small creek bed just below Old Hollow Top Mountain he found real gold, lots of dust and several nuggets. Seizing his long-sought chance to shout, he found a partner to help wash the gravels of his new claim. But steady work held few charms for the little fellow and he moved on to what he hoped would be even more glittering chances to shout.

He left very little of himself at the creek. The others who moved in to take advantage of the finds could not even remember his name. Was it Tecumseh Smith? One man was sure that was it. Another said, no, it was the other way around — Smith Tecumseh. Still another insisted it was not Tecumseh at all but McCumpsey. Then somebody remembered the little guy answered to "Pony" and that stuck. The diminutive wanderer, although vanished to other parts, left his nickname attached to a creek, a gulch and what would be a booming mining camp.

In a couple of years after Pony's finds, the gulch was full of men working the gravels with pans, rockers and cradles. Water was in short supply, turning into a muddy soup as it was used over and over again. Then about 1870 George Hadzor and J. C. Hawkins built a combination flume and ditch from neighboring Cataract Creek, bringing in so much water the placer beds were soon worked out.

Searching the hills for the lode which must have been the source of gold supply, George Moreland found the out-cropping in the middle of a patch of wild strawberries. He dug down about fourteen feet and there uncovered his bonanza, ore worth all the way from $20,000 to $100,000 a ton. The claim immediately below Moreland's Strawberry was full of chunks of rocks so thick with gold it could be mashed out with a pestle.

The rush was quick to swell the population of Strawberry to several hundred and it soon had a post office, store and the usual jerry-built saloons. Moreland had acquired several good claims close by, one of them the Crevice, and close to the mine he built a mill which added to the prosperity of the little boom camp.

The town of Pony itself began to take solid form with the erection of a five-stamp mill which had been knocked down and moved from Sterling by the Mallory brothers in 1875. The little mill was soon swamped by rich ores being dug close by and was augmented by another five-stamper, this moved in from the failing Rising Mill in Norwegian Gulch. Reconstruction was hastily done during the winter, one of the Mallory brothers slipping on ice while carrying a timber and falling to his death.

By 1876 Pony had eclipsed the earlier camp of Strawberry which became merely a suburb, yet in taking two steps forward Pony went back one. The first boom was showing signs of fading when a new burst of activity came in '77, adding another 1,000 in population, several new buildings and a dwindling of ore reserves. Then newer discoveries around Phillipsburg caused a second relapse and Pony was down to a small handful again. Another few

2 PONY'S mines lay idle for many years before persistent hopes for reactivation died. Some remained on standby basis, ready to start at almost moment's notice, others, partly dismantled would need additional equipment.

years and some of the fresh discoveries proved to be bubbles and Pony's more modest diggins looked good once again. The Tobacco Root camp now settled down to its best years, producing steadily if not spectacularly. Such mines as the Boss Tweed, Clipper, Bell, Eclipse, Charity and Summit were turning out hundreds of thousands of dollars in gold ore to be crushed in the many mills around Pony.

A more conventional ghost has been reported seen by Mrs. Hill. She was walking near her home one moonlit night when she was alerted by the barking of her dogs. She saw the shadowy figure of a man walking slowly toward the Grant House, the one-time stage station. As the spectre approached the rear of the building, where legend says a treasure is buried, it vanished. Mrs. Hill found later that several people had reported the same visitation, in each case the ghost disappearing just as it reached the treasure site. Her research

also revealed a story that the supposed treasure had once inspired a Mexican to search the spot, having arrived in town with a map. He tried digging in the only place behind the old station which was not solid rock. At a depth of several feet he unearthed an ancient high-counter boot. He replaced the relic and fled the scene with no explanation. Residents at that time said a murdered witness had been buried along with the treasure.

And then there was the haunt that frequently visited the old spring flowing near the original stage station. This one gave off a "dancing light" and was an accustomed sight to townsmen. Then came the severe earthquake in the spring of 1887 when shifting of the earth's crust destroyed the flow of water in the spring. The water-loving phantom was never seen again but Shakespeare could easily spare a ghost or two and never miss them.

Business houses flourished during the decade. Paul Taft and Potter's Livery Stable, Isdell's and

173

Cramer's stores, Gilbert's Saloon —all doing well. It was said the swinging doors at Gilbert's never stopped flapping. One of Pony's merchants was the druggist, William H. Morris who, with Henry Elling, bought and operated the Boss Tweed-Clipper combination which produced $5 million. Morris had been a druggist in Virginia City before coming to Pony. While his new store there was being built the Vigilantes used an exposed beam to string up five of Henry Plummer's henchmen.

Several things happened in rapid succession at the turn of the century, events that seemed to be launching Pony into big time mining. The Boss Tweed, Clipper and other mines produced well through the '90s but were showing signs of failing in values of ore produced in 1900. That year Henry Elling died and partner Morris offered the property for sale. A Boston syndicate sent a team of mining experts to examine the properties. They went over the ground, descended shafts, pecked at ore dumps and estimated there was easily $10 million worth of ore in the combined mines.

The Eastern concern immediately clinched the deal and set about development in a big way. First it bought a hundred-stamp mill and set it up at Pony. It was operated by electricity, a modern innovation, and in connection were large cyanide tanks for ore reduction. Not until then was the undeniably large supply of ore sampled for values and availability — and found to be of low grade, suitable for roasting methods only. The Boston men folded their tents and stole away without ever stamping a ton of ore. Morris returned from California and took over the property again. He continued to put the ore through his old twenty-stamp mill, making a moderate profit in his remaining years. He died in 1904.

The sale of the mine properties to the eastern concern had the effect of stimulating interest in other mines in the area and for a time Pony enjoyed a period of prosperity not too badly affected by the cyanide plant fiasco. A brick school house costing $12,000 was built. An Episcopal Church was erected but services were spasmodic, the Reverend Lewis blaming the weather for scant attendance. A small Catholic edifice held Mass on special occasions. A Presbyterian church was built in 1894, finally becoming a community church.

In October of 1918, James L. Linn, now of Portland, moved to Pony. Although only thirteen years old at the time he has many memories of the camp. "I went there with my father, Leslie Linn,

who worked for the Copeland Lumber Yard there. Mr. Copeland was a brother of J. W. Copeland who now has lumber yards scattered over the west, particularly in Nevada. There were still many signs of past mining around the town. In fact lots of the mill buildings and shaft houses looked as though they could start up again the next day. One big stamp mill had no machinery at all, just the huge 4½-foot fir blocks where the stamps could be set. Possibly it was just a big promotional hoax." (The author is almost certain these were the remains of the mill so hopefully built by the Boston syndicate in 1900).

"There were about 300 people in Pony at the time," says James Linn, "including a number of boys about my age. We used to make lots of short trips around the hills close to town, exploring the old mine shafts, a very dangerous business as I look back. But we learned a lot about mining. We hiked up toward Old Hollow Top Mountain and came to the old camp of Strawberry. It was completely abandoned and the old buildings falling down.

"We got one of the old timers to identify the mines for us. The Clipper was one of the largest and was still getting out gold." (The author concludes from a report of William Barnett, also now of Portland, manager of the Copeland yard after Linn, that the Clipper mine was in its last days of production, as he says all mines in Pony were closed in 1922). "Our guide told us the Boss Tweed mine had produced $2 million in the old days. He said it had the largest system of untimbered stopes in the world and added that they were perfectly safe, being cut out of solid granite."

"The town was still fairly active. The blacksmith shop still had a pile of coal beside the forge, ready to go, it seemed. The old bunkhouse was still well stocked with food that would keep, like canned goods, and the kitchen was still equipped with cooking utensils. The old bank built by Mr. Morris was run by a Mr. Smith, who kept his big Kissel Car parked out in front all the time. We were told he would be glad to keep your money safe, but wouldn't pay you any interest.

"He took us to what used to be one of the saloons. It had a board walk in front, full of cracks between the boards. He said that when the town was in its prime a bunch of miners would gather there and take turns pitching twenty dollar gold pieces at a certain crack, not as wide then as now. When one man's lucky throw placed the gold piece exactly centered on the line, he took the whole pot."

NEW MEXICO

SHAKESPEARE, NEW MEXICO

It was Christmas of 1882 in Shakespeare and the town was celebrating with a big community party. The tree was a symmetrical pine brought down from the mountains. It was lavishly decorated, most of the ornaments home-made but not the most conspicuous one. This was a doll, about two and a half feet tall with arms and legs of cloth, a sawdust body and head of china, the prized possession of eight-year-old Emma Marble. She had brought it from Virginia City, Nevada, when she came with her mother and sister to join her father who had established a home for them in the raw mining camp.

The doll was admired by everyone, especially little Jane, the daughter of Mr. and Mrs. Nick Hughes. Jane could not take her wide eyes from the china beauty and talked of it all the way home. Not long afterward she fell ill and in her delirium constantly called for the doll. Her sister Mary went to the Marble home and asked Emma if she could take the doll to Jane, offering a five dollar gold piece for the favor. It was gladly granted and Jane had her doll — for a few days. When she died she was placed in a simple board coffin and her arms tightly clutched the doll with the china head. The coffin was placed in the little cemetery already holding so many who had met tragic or violent death in the camp.

Two of the cemetery's occupants were Pony Express riders slain by renegade Indians under Cochise and Geronimo. The site of what would be Shakespeare was decided by the presence of a good spring a few miles from the site of Lordsburg. The Butterfield Stage Station called Barney had been nearby, failing when the Butterfield Lines met disaster from effects of the Civil War. As soon as it ended a new line called the National was established and John Evensen was sent out to refurbish the station, now called Pyramid after the nearby range of mountains. The next name change came when Evensen, impressed by the current popularity of General Grant, bestowed the officer's name on the tiny group of adobe buildings. A year later the county was also named Grant.

About this time a government survey party, of which one member was W. B. Brown, was working in the area. Brown was a prospector at heart, not vitally interested in surveying, so the rocky ground received more attention than did his transit with the result that he found a spectacular specimen crisscrossed with veins of silver. He deserted the survey party and rushed to San Francisco with the sample.

A believer in going straight to the top man, Brown obtained an interview with Bank or California magnate William C. Ralston simply by showing his chunk of silver ore. Although Ralston was fighting Adolph Sutro's attempts to bore a tunnel to the bottom of Virginia City's mines, he was not too absorbed to overlook a good thing in Brown's offer of a partnership in exchange for capital to develop the New Mexico silver property. The financier personally had the ore sample assayed and when results showed 12,000 ounces of silver to the ton he formed a company to stake out further claims and set up a mining district to be called the Virginia Mining District with the little stage station as its center. With the consequent influx of workers and drifters a town soon developed at the hub and was rechristened Ralston.

The company made a miserable attempt to recover values and quickly failed. Blame was placed partly on absentee ownership, Ralston being too busy with Bank of California interests in the fading Virginia City to pay much attention to a far

away New Mexico mine. Then Ralston's bank was forced to close its doors in the financial panic and Ralston resigned as officer of the bank. He went out for his customary swim in cold San Francisco Bay, was apparently seized with cramps and drowned, some sources claiming it was suicide. With this event the town and the nine-by-four mile mining district in the Pyramids took a new name, that of the new owners, the Shakespeare Co., a concession to a large block of British stockholders. One of the two little adobe hotels was also named Shakespeare and a most natural title of Stratford House settled on the other.

The town was subjected to many short booms and sharp declines, the result of over-promotion. An editorial in the MINING NEWS, July 26, 1881, said

LOOKING DOWN AVON AVENUE from intersecting old stage road. Long unused branch line of Southern Pacific runs along middle of street. Tin version of "covered wagon" stands bereft of wheels at left. Behind is old saloon. Right is Grant House, then Stratford Hotel where George W. Hunt, late great Governor of Arizona waited table as youth. At right, on near side of street is General Store.

camp have begun to realize this fact and have thrown aside the puffing policy and gone to work in earnest."

F. Stanley, New Mexico historian, gives a vivid picture of the place in his SHAKESPEARE STORY: "The houses were built of adobe. The walls were thick to withstand Indian attacks, the windows small so they could be boarded up in a hurry. Victorio and his warriors were still making the rounds during the early days of Shakespeare history. The town was unique among mining towns of New Mexico, if not the Southwest, for it boasted no plumbing, no club, no church, no school, no fraternal organization, no bank. Even the dance hall girls who came in from Deming and Lordsburg were permitted neither residence or domicile in Shakespeare. The same carriage that brought them also took them back the same night."

Later no doubt, when the town had reached its peak of about 3,000 people, such extreme restrictions on the girls' activities were relaxed with the opening of Roxy Jay's Saloon. Its bar ran the length of the building, the longest adobe in the area. Made of polished mahogany, it was brought from St. Louis,

FRANK HILL LEANS against door frame of first building on site of Shakespeare, already there when stage station was erected. Frank has been horse wrangler all his life. "Rita and I bought the ranch, including the town of Shakespeare in 1935", he says. "We intended to make a living with horses, but you have to break a horse every day, and I'm getting too old for that. Now we just want to keep the historic old town in shape and entertain visitors." Hills charge small fee to admit and guide those interested.

of the situation: "Work at Shakespeare is being pushed ahead systematically. Shakespeare has had no little to contend against. When the district was first opened up it was puffed and lauded to the skies by a series of mining speculators who wished to dispose of their claims before doing any work to show there was anything in them to warrant investment by capitalists. . . . The mine owners of this

DINING ROOM of Grant House, scene of hanging of Russian Bill and Sandy King. When management offered no such diversions as cutting down bodies, diners amused selves shooting at flies on wall.

part way by eighteen-mule freight wagon. Also freighted in, and even more precariously, was the wonder of the town, an enormous mirror for the back bar. It was held in such awe and respect by habituees that although the doors were so full of bullet holes "they look like lacework", the mirror was never hit by flying lead.

Although Shakespeare was considered to be an extremely "honest town", one prominent citizen known to keep as much as $30,000 in a baking powder can, there was no lack of excitement. Most deeds of violence were perpetrated by out of towners. Frequent raids and shooting scrapes occurred when such "prominent" personalities as Curly Bill, Johnny Ringo, Dave Rudabaugh, Sandy King and Russian Bill came to town. The activities of these gunmen were so frequent the nerves of citizens finally snapped into action. They organized the Shakespeare Guards which were recognized by the Territorial Government in 1879. The Guards summary treatment of two of the more persistent tor-

mentors was followed by several peaceful years.

One was Russian Bill, fugitive from Russia where, as Count Feador Telfrin, member of the Imperial Guards, he had been involved in some shady money deals. Fleeing to Arizona he went to work on the McLowery ranch and also became associated with the equally notorious Clantons. Finding himself without a horse near the Speer ranch one day, he took one, but was spotted by a ranch hand. Apprehended in Deming, Russian Bill was brought to Shakespeare's shiny new jail which had been heralded in the Santa Fe NEW MEXICAN on September 28, 1881: "Shakespeare is to have a substantial calaboose. Its cost is estimated to be about four hundred dollars."

Flung into this proud structure, Russian Bill found he was not in solitary. One Sandy King had the honor of being the jug's first guest. Sandy had refused to pay for a gaudy silk handkerchief in Smyth's haberdashery, then literally added injury to insult by whipping out his six-shooter and

ORIGINAL MAIL STATION, established about 1856 at Mexican Springs forerunner of later Shakespeare. Roof was constructed of dead Yucca bloom-stocks closely laid then plastered with clay and brush.

179

clipping off the index finger of the clerk's outstretched hand.

The NEW MEXICAN reported the events that followed: "You doubtless have heard of Russian Bill and Sandy King, two noted horse thieves and desperados. They were brought to Shakespeare a few days ago and lodged in jail. Yesterday they were loud and demonstrative against the citizens, declaring that the people of the town would have a chance to dance to their music in twenty-four days. During the small hours of the night the jail was visited by an armed force, the guard was overpowered and in an hour or so two pulseless bodies, stiff and cold, could be seen suspended by a cord to a girder in what was formerly the barroom of the old Shakespeare Hotel . . . Shakespeare is on its mettle and woe betide the unfortunate who raises the next row at this place. A coroner's jury ruled that the men met death by suicide."

Other reports fill in some details lacking in the newspaper statement. The reason the beam in the room was selected as a gallows was the scarcity of trees. The bodies were not cut down immediately. A large number of passengers was expected on the noon stage and it seemed a shame to deprive them of the edifying spectacle, so the bodies were left in place until after their arrival. One of the passengers offered to help carry the body of Russian Bill to the cemetery in exchange for the fine boots he wore. He said he thought they would fit him and they did. A final note was sounded by the NEW MEXICAN a few days later. "Shakespeare has not been annoyed by ruffians since the last necktie party. The friends of the two men who were lynched there a week or so ago have not avenged the death of their comrades as they threatened to. There is nothing that lessens the zeal of the average desperado than a conscientious vigilante committee." This story of Russian Bill's demise differs sharply from one credited to a member of the School of Mines at Socorro. (See GHOST TOWN ALBUM).

Then there was the affair involving the handsome "Arkansaw". Young Robert Black, who bore the nickname because he had come from that state, was carrying on an affair with the wife of a prominent citizen of the town, the outraged husband said, when he urged the vigilantes to action. They

GRANT HOUSE. Old stage station and dining room was named when whole town was called Grant for Civil War general. Windows were unusually large for day, more cheerful than most, but presented hazard in times of Indian attacks. Supply of rocks was kept piled inside under windows, stacked on sills in case of raid, providing protection from arrows, holes for extending rifles.

were reluctant but finally the wandering Romeo was caught and given the rope treatment. His feet had just left the ground when the saloon keeper, Roxy Jay, grieved at an obvious waste of an efficient mine worker, called out: "He's too good a man to hang. Let the woman and her husband get out of town."

Hangings and near hangings were interspersed with sporadic Indian raids, most of them without fatalities. At each alarm however, one of the women, Mrs. W. D. Griffith, would rush to the closet where she kept her treasured wig. She said that if and when she was scalped the Apache would get her "falsie" and not her own locks.

Ghosts have made their presence known in Shakespeare where in most deserted towns they remain secluded. Several spectres have become familiar through reported appearances, one preferring to attract attention to his sulphurous aroma. This one "lives" in the basement of the adobe residence of Mr. and Mrs. Frank Hill, used as a school about 1905. During a lunch hour the children amused themselves by digging in the dirt floor of the basement, unearthing a number of bones which the teacher identified as human and ordered them reburied immediately. Since then, at intervals of several months, the ghost comes upstairs, companionably emitting faint sulphur fumes "like the odor of a struck match."

SHAKESPEARE CEMETERY (opposite page) has been preempted by Mexicans from Lordsburg. Graves are decked with paper flowers fluttering in breeze. Burial ground contains remains of Russian Bill and Sandy King, lynch victims "dumped in the same hole", tiny body of Jane Hughes, her arms cradling the china doll, her grave unmarked but next to uncle's, James Hughes, bearing weathered marker. Sharp peak in background is Lee's Peak, called Mt. Aera during heyday of Shakespeare, and scene of fantastic "Diamond Hoax." Actual diamonds were "salted" on peak to be found by wildly enthusiastic prospective buyers of stock in San Francisco and New York Mining and Commercial Co. Diamond craze added to population of booming Shakespeare, swelling figure to 3000 in 1872. Hoax was perpetrated during days of William Ralston's control, exposure was said to contribute to circumstances leading to his supposed suicide in San Francisco Bay.

PONCHA SPRINGS, COLORADO

Although Poncha Springs owed its big development of the mining boom in the late 1870s it was already established as a health resort several years previously. At the site are 99 mineral springs, their temperatures varying from 90 to 185 degrees. The Utes and other Indians had been in the habit of camping here from prehistoric times, claiming that the waters of Poncha Springs were "Good Medicine."

One of the earliest whites in the region was a Mr. McPherson, who had a homesteading claim near the largest springs. In 1874 James True bought the claim and laid out a town. He started a general store which became a bonanza when the rush of miners hit the area. When the railroad came through in 1880 Poncha Springs enjoyed a boom undreamed of by the first settlers. Several hotels were quickly put up including the Jackson which still stands, though greatly altered. It was operated by a retired Memphis steamboat captain, and saw some wild times while the railroad was being extended and trackworkers and crewmen swarmed the town.

In her "Stampede to Timberline" Muriel Wolle quotes the CHAFFEE COUNTY TIMES of January 1, 1881 as saying "The prohibition tendency of the

principal owners of town property has caused them to insert a clause in all deeds prohibiting the sale of intoxicating liquor on any lots belonging to them, and the consequence is a small proportion of saloons to other classes of business. We believe there are only two or three in the town. How many drugstores and groceries have private barrels on tap cannot be definitely stated."

There was also a library, a novelty in any boom camp, "a neat, cozy building, containing over 1600 standard volumes and a large number of choice novels, including selections from Harper's half hour series." . . . . . . "This will be a great boon for the army of strangers, young men and others, who, in coming to this mountain town will be provided with a profitable place to spend their evenings instead of frequenting saloons and dancehouses."

Proper or not, Poncha Springs flourished for only a few years, being almost entirely destroyed by fire in 1882. The town was never rebuilt, the boom resulting from building of the railroad having subsided. The Jackson Hotel and the large brick schoolhouse remain as landmarks.

ONCE ELEGANT SCHOOLHOUSE served children of booming Poncha Springs until fire in 1882 laid waste town already failing. Building was isolated by conflagration, is now surrounded by huge cottonwoods and locusts.

SHAVANO, COLORADO

"Colorado, Its Gold and Silver Mines", published in 1880, has this to say of the mining district straddling the Monarch Pass. "Monarch mining district is located around the headwaters of the South Arkansas river in the southwestern corner of the county. Many of the lodes are above timberline. A district as young as this that can show such promising and valuable mines as the Mountain Chief, Monarch, Smith and Gray, Songbird and Gulch is sure to take a front rank now that the railroad has reached the neighborhood. The towns of the Monarch district are Maysville, Arbourville and Chaffee. The latter is up among the mines and the former nearer the base of the mountain and seem to be the business points. Maysville is 13 miles from the railroad at Cleora, 6 from the mineral springs at Poncho and 8 miles below Monarch Mountain and Chaffee.

"Around the middle fork of the South Arkansas the ore is almost entirely of carbonate of lead or galena, the former predominating. Fine specimens

MARKER INFORMS RARE VISITORS, mostly fishermen that here once stood flourishing Colorado mining camp. Tortuous, steep road winds 7 miles from Maysville on highway at approach to Monarch Pass, is not recommended for average traveler. Side road, not used since mining days leaves at right for Shavano mines, above timberline. Mountain meadows still bore winter's snow drifts at time of photographer's visit, soon to be replaced by sheets of alpine flowers.

of chlorides and silver glance are, however, not entirely wanting, and sometimes the ore is enriched by chlorides to such an extent that it would not be difficult to sort out considerable quantities that would mill out over a thousand ounces to the ton."

It was just such a deposit of galena ore that came to light at the location first called Clifton, seven miles above Maysville. The camp was started in 1879 and was laid out as a town the next year. While the ore was mostly galena, heavy with lead, there was just enough easily recovered silver to sustain optimism and even promote a small boom. Any newcomer was welcome to wood, water and a twenty-five foot building site on the main "street", so long as he cleared and graded his frontage. All buildings were constructed of logs. They formed a double line straggling along a rough thoroughfare which crossed the wildly cascading Cyclone Creek on a timbered bridge.

The creek made a right-angle turn a quarter of a mile below the street, paralleling it, and in a comparatively gentle mood formed a ford where another road could cross. Just below the crossing a three story mill was built, and an access road graded up the steep mountainside to the mines.

It was the fashion at the time to name mining camps after prominent Indian chiefs, and a movement was started in Clifton to rename the camp for the famous leader, Ouray. Then it was found that Ouray was already thus honored, so the town on Cyclone Creek took second choice, the name of Shavano, a sub-chief under Ouray. Although not having the linguistic abilities of the great Ouray who spoke Spanish and English, Shavano was tactful, often presiding at meetings in Ouray's absence.

Re-naming the town was hardly worth the trouble, the vein of lead with some silver rapidly became all lead as it was followed, then not even that. Shavano folded in only a little more than three years of glory, its log cabins and stores already abandoned.

ONLY STANDING BUILDING in 11,000' high Shavano is still partly roofed with sheet metal, contains crude bedstead and other comforts of home. Although picture was taken in mid-June, snow was pelting down, flakes not registering in one second exposure required by red filter and heavily overcast early morning sky. Trip down narrow, rugged, dirt road was accomplished in increasingly heavy snowstorm, which abated only when 9,000' level was reached.

About twenty years later a rich vein of silver was located still farther up the range, the find being made by a Shavano man, Judge J. H. Akin and E. W. Carpenter of Salida. Although it was New Year's Day and three feet of snow covered the ground the men staked out a claim on the spot, calling it the Netsie Castley. A 200 pound sample chunk of rock from this vein contained 119 ounces of silver, a hefty portion of lead and gold assaying $3.50 to the ton.

The discovery revived Shavano as a supply base while the mine was being developed. However, the new vein, while rich, didn't last any longer than the lower one, and after a few years it too was abandoned.

Today, Shavano is almost gone. Only one cabin still stands, and that because a tin roof has preserved it from rotting and collapse. A careful survey through the woods at the site reveals about twenty sites where buildings once stood. Most had stone fireplaces at one end. Considerable care was used in smoothing logs for door and window sills and in placing pegs for shelf supports. In a few years the logs in contact with the ground will complete the rotting process, dissolving into the rocky earth and disappearing completely.

BUENA VISTA, COLORADO

The new railroad had reached only as far as Buena Vista and passengers for the loudly booming silver camps of Leadville and Aspen had to change to stages at that point. This situation soon created still another mushroom metropolis, Buena Vista itself which quickly took its place among a succession of camps claiming the honor of "the most lawless town in the West."

Among the dozens of saloons that sprouted along the single street was one bawdy place with a hastily scrawled sign across its false front — The Mule Skinner's Retreat. A door or two away was the tiny post office and a problem soon developed for the buxom lady serving as postmistress. A sizeable element in the town was "on the lam", drifters operating under a number of aliases. The lady of letters agreed to drop all mail for such names in a special box at the back window which had a pane missing, the questionable characters to reach through and take what they wanted.

The most vivid description of Buena Vista in those days was written by a traveler named Ingham for a book, DIGGING GOLD AMONG THE ROCKIES, published in 1880. He said: "Buena Vista is a new town situated near the headwaters of the Arkansas river. This town five months ago had only three buildings, it now contains from three to four hundred cheap wooden structures, some well built hotels, saloons and gambling houses without number. It claims a population of 1500. The town is in the midst of a park country, surrounded on all sides by magnificent snow-covered mountains. A little southwest is Mount Princeton, rising grandly to a height of 14,196 feet, and a number of other peaks raise their white summits almost as high.

"Tents greet the eye along the streets in every direction. Large canvas covered buildings, tents filled with merchandise and mammoth tents transformed into warehouses crammed full of freight supplies en route to Leadville and the Gunnison country are everywhere seen.

At the depot we saw seven four-horse stage coaches loading with passengers for Leadville, be-

sides other vehicles taking in passengers for Alpine, Pitkin and Gunnison City. Eight, and sometimes nine persons are crammed inside the Concord Coaches which look as if four persons would be a sufficient load inside — while four or even five persons are put on top of the box. The fare to Leadville from Buena Vista is $5 for a distance of thirty-four miles. Six and eight mule freight teams, hauling two canvas covered wagons, one hitched closely behind the other, laden with freight

BRIGHT RED BUILDING is one of many still in use in Buena Vista and dating from days of silver rush. Town was founded in 1879 by prospectors, becoming metropolis overnight as temporary end of rail line eventually completed to Leadville. During boom period Buena Vista became headquarters of bunco men, gamblers and prostitutes, situation became intolerable to "respectable element" of town, vigilantes hanged some of most notorious crooks, drove rest out of town.

OLD COURT HOUSE bears unique weather-vane. Buena Vista became county seat of Chaffee County later in same year of founding. Granite, former seat was unwilling to give up records, committee of Buena Vista citizens chartered locomotive and flat car, removed records at night from hiding place from loft above brewery in Granite.

of all kinds for Leadville, jacks and mules loaded with their packs for Gunnison were constantly moving out. At the depot tons upon tons of base bullion, (silver and lead), in bars (or pigs) from fifty to one hundred pounds each were closely piled upon the platform for fifty feet in length, which was fairly broken down with the great weight it bore. These bear the stamp of permanent smelters, and are being shipped east, where the silver will be separated from the lead.

"Buena Vista has been a lively town for the past four months, being the terminus of the Denver and Rio Grande Railway, the nearest station to Leadville. But the line will have completed a road up the Arkansas from Canon City past this place to Leadville by July 1st, when this place will have to decline.

"The buildings here, as we stated before, are of the most temporary nature except a few of them. The hotel where we stopped was plastered with building paper tacked to the walls, and ceiled and whitewashed overhead with thin white muslin fastened in the same manner. We got good accommodations, however, and were well fed for two dollars a day. Some hotels, though, ask three."

The town today retains much of the old flavor, the mountains still form the background, many of the old buildings remain in good condition.

ROLL CALL OF THE SHADOWS

Publisher's note: The listing makes no pretense of being complete. As this is being written both Mr. Florin and Dr. Mason are in the field photographing and researching the material for additional works to supplement *Western Ghost Towns*, *Ghost Town Album*, *Ghost Town Trails*, and this book *Ghost Town Shadows*, the fourth in the series.

Towns in large type are treated either in *Western Ghost Towns*, *Ghost Town Album*, *Ghost Town Trails*, or *Ghost Town Shadows* as indicated. Those in small type are candidates for future publications and are listed for the benefit of the reader who may wish to investigate them himself.

ALASKA

Ghost Town Shadows—Skagway

Anvil Creek, Tanana, Crooked Creek, Eagle, Chicken (Ptarmigan), Jack Wade, Ketchumstuck.

ARIZONA

Western Ghost Towns — Chloride, Goldroad, Oatman, Whitehills.
Ghost Town Album—Tombstone, Gleason.
Ghost town Trails—Mineral Park, Jerome.
Ghost Town Shadows — McCabe, Bumblebee, Stanton, Congress, Octave, Crown King, Weaver.

Salome, Quartzite, Vulture City, Tubac, Charleston, Millville, Fairbanks, Dos Cabezas, Mowrey, Pearce, Ehrenberg, La Paz, Metcalf, Constellation.

BRITISH COLUMBIA

Ghost Town Trails — Beaver Pass, Richfield, Barkerville, Cameronton, Stanley, Yale, Ashcroft Manor, Copper Mountain, Allenby, Granite Creek, Hedley, Coalmont.

Ghost Town Shadows—Bennet Lake.
Wardley, Atlin, Waldo, Baynes, Ft. Steele, Poplar, Phoenix, Baynes, Zincton, Silverton, Fisherville, Warnell, Lumberton, Wardner.

CALIFORNIA

Western Ghost Towns—Ballarat, Bodie, Cerro Gordo, Darwin, Masonic, Swansea, Calico.
Ghost Town Album—Mariposa, Hornitos, Bear Valley, Sawmill Flats, Columbia, Sonora, Jamestown, Jackson, Vallecito, Murphys, Altaville, Mokelumne Hill, Volcano, Fiddletown.
Ghost Town Trails — Coloma, Rough and Ready, Sierra City, Downieville, North San Juan, Grass Valley, Nevada City, Timbuctoo.
Ghost Town Shadows — Weaverville, Douglas City, Whiskeytown, Old Shasta, French Gulch.

Hawkinsville, Paradise, Panamint, Nortonville, Empire, West Hartley, Judsonville, Knob, Sommersville, Randsburg.

COLORADO

Western Ghost Towns—Animas Forks, Eureka, Gladstone, Kokomo, St. Elmo, Leadville, Silverton.

Ghost Town Album — Cripple Creek, Victor, Lake City, Bonanza, Villa Grove, Crestone, Creede.

Ghost Town Trails—Alma, Breckenridge, Fairplay, Silver Plume, Georgetown, Blackhawk, Central City, Apex, Ward.

Ghost Town Shadows — Maysville, Shavano, Buena Vista, Poncha Springs.

Pitkin, Crested Butte, Gothic, Jack's Cabin, Iola, White Pine, Tomichi Creek, Crystal, Romley, Telluride, Marble, Ashcroft, Tincup.

IDAHO

Western Ghost Towns — Burke, Gem, Idaho City, Murray, Pioneerville, Placerville, Potosi Gulch, Silver City.

Ghost Town Album — Leesburg, Shoup, Bayhorse.

Atlanta, Warren, Delamarr, Custer, Clayton, Rocky Bar, Triumph, Bitch Creek.

MONTANA

Western Ghost Towns—Bannack, Bearmouth, Beartown, Clancey, Elkhorn, Garnet, Granite, Keystone, Laurin, Mammoth, Marysville, Melrose, Philipsburg, Rimini, Southern Cross, Virginia City, Wickes.

Ghost Town Album—Giltedge, Kendall, Maiden.

Ghost Town Trails—Castle City.
Ghost Town Shadows—Pony.

Landusky, Chester, Hecla, Yogo Gulch, Copperopolis, Confederate Gulch, Grizzly Gulch, Louisville, Pioneer, Norris, Ruby, Emigrant Gulch, Greenhorn.

NEVADA

Western Ghost Towns—Austin, Belmont, Candelaria, Dayton, Eureka, Fairview, Galena, Goldpoint, Goldfield, Goodsprings, Hamilton, Manhattan, Midas, Tuscarora, Nelson, Pine Grove, Rhyolite, Rochester, Tonopah, Unionville, Virginia City.

Ghost Town Album—Washoe, National.

Ghost Town Trails—Genoa.

Ghost Town Shadows—Broken Hills, Rawhide, Rockland, Aurora, Ione, Grantsville, Berlin.

Paradise, Shafter, Golconda, Jarbridge, Jefferson, Osceola, Pioche, Rio Tinto, Mountain City, Goldcreek, Charleston.

NEW MEXICO

Ghost Town Album — Tyrone, Magdalena, Kelly, White Oaks, Kingston, Lake Valley, Hillsboro, Pinos Altos.

Ghost Town Trails — Alma, Mogollon, Elizabethtown.

Ghost Town Shadows—Shakespeare.

Colmor, Dawson, Organ, Cimarron, Folsom, Koehler, Brilliant, Gardiner, Watrous, Colfax, Madrid, Hatch, Cabezon, Georgetown.

OREGON

Western Ghost Towns—Antelope, Austin, Bonanza, Bourne, Cornucopia, Granite, Grandview, Greenhorn, Hardman, Hoskins, Jacksonville, Kerby, Marysville, Shaniko, Sumpter, Whitney.

Ghost Town Album—Auburn, Malheur City, Lonerock, Richmond, Sanger.

Ghost Town Trails—Paisley, Mabel, Ashwood, Shelburn.

Ghost Town Shadows — Kings Valley, Chitwood, Kernville, Elk City.

New Era, Aurora, Butteville, Wheatland, Buena Vista, Champoeg, Ortley, Wauna, Goble, Natal, Mist, Apiary, Paulina, St. Louis, Sweden, Niagara, Susanville, Hugo, Galice.

SOUTH DAKOTA

Ghost Town Album—Cascade Springs, Custer, Hill City.

Ghost Town Trails—Crook City, Central City, Lead, Terry, Pluma, Preston, Trojan, Deadwood.

Ghost Town Shadows — Galena, Sheridan, Rochford, Rockerville.

Evarts, Travare, Le Beau, Witten, Cater, Wheeler, Milltown, Tinton, Dakota City, Rockport, Haward, City, Bon Homme, Fairbank, Palisade, Parade, La Foon.

UTAH

Ghost Town Album—Bingham Canyon, Alta, Mammoth, Park City, Eureka, Silver City.

Ghost Town Trails—Iosepa, Mercur.

Ghost Town Shadows—Corinne.

Sego, Standardville, Gold Hill, Fairfield, Silver Reef, Grafton, Spring Canyon, Hiawatha.

WASHINGTON

Western Ghost Towns—Blewett Pass, Copper City, Index, Liberty, Skamokawa, Sultan, Trinity, Wilkeson.

Ghost Town Album—Northport, Bossburg, Republic, Orient, Curlew.

Ghost Town Trails — Riverside, Nighthawk, Loomis, Ruby, Conconully.

Ghost Town Shadows — Port Ludlow, Port Gamble, Home Colony, Union.

Monte Cristo, Frankfort, Naselle, Knappton, Brookfield, McGowan, Altoona, Deep River, Garland Springs, Holden, Pluvius, Oysterville, Metzger.

WYOMING

Western Ghost Towns — Atlantic City, South Pass City, Diamondville.

Ghost Town Album—Encampment Battle Rambler.

Ghost Town Trails—Medicine Bow.

Ghost Town Shadows—Opal, Glencoe.

Carbon, Du Noir, Dennison, Gold Hill, Miners' Delight, Viola.

YUKON TERRITORY

Ghost Town Shadows — Dawson City, Louse Town, Carmacks, Carcross, Closeleigh.

Clear Creek, Forty-Mile, Elsa, Gordon Landing, Dalton Post.

OLD GENERAL STORE built on rock foundation and with good roof has stood ravages of time better than most buildings in town, is now home of Hills and daughter Janaloo. Several Chinese were once killed in store to avoid payment of wages due them for work on railroad. Rita Hill thinks the bones unearthed in basement by school children may have been Celestials. Building faces on Avon Avenue, looking toward Arroyo de Los Negros. Latter was named for two negros who owned mine property, usually had money, were invited to gamble in crooked game in saloon of Grant House. Negros won, instead, were pursued up gulch by angry operators and killed.